P9-CRZ-807

Feathered Serpent

By the same author

The Land and People of Central America
Neighbors in a New World: The Organization of American States
The Seven Worlds of Peru
Hello Guatemala
Brazil Today
Song of the Quail: The Wondrous World of the Maya
Kingdom of the Sun: The Inca, Empire Builders of the Americas

Feathered Serpent
The Rise and Fall of the Aztecs

by

RUTH KAREN

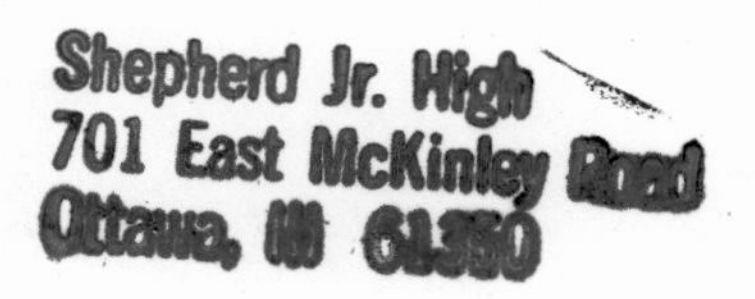

FOUR WINDS PRESS NEW YORK

Grateful acknowledgment is made to the following authors and publishers for the use of copyrighted materials. Every effort has been made to obtain permission to use previously published material. Any errors or ommissions are unintentional.

Doubleday & Co., Inc. for the excerpts from *The Bernal Diaz Chronicles*, translated and edited by Albert Idell, copyright © 1956 by Albert Idell.

Faber & Faber, Ltd. for the excerpts from *Firefly in the Night* by Irene Nicholson, copyright © 1959 by Irene Nicholson.

The University of Utah Press for the excerpts from *A General History of the Things of New Spain*, edited and translated by Charles E. Dibble and Arthur J.O. Anderson.

All photographs courtesy of the Instituto Nacional de Antropologia e Historia, Mexico City. The illustrations on pages iii, iv, v, 1, 3, 15, 37, 66, 78, 107, 137, 141, 165 are from Design Motifs of Ancient Mexico *by Jorge Encisco, courtesy Dover Publications, Inc. The map and illustrations on pages vii, 49, 94, 143, 167, 176, 180 are by Lucy Martin Bitzer.*

LIBRARY OF CONGRESS CATALOGING IN PUBLICATION DATA

Karen, Ruth.
Feathered serpent.
Bibliography: p.
Includes index.
1. Aztecs—History. I. Title.
F1219.K29 972 78-22129
ISBN 0-590-07413-X

Published by Four Winds Press
A division of Scholastic Magazines, Inc., New York, N.Y.

Printed in the United States of America
Library of Congress Catalog Card Number: 78-22129
5 4 3 2 1 83 82 81 80 79

Contents

ANÁHUAC

The Aztec Empire

PART ONE

CHAPTER ONE

The Subway Stop of the Curled Snake

THE gleaming new subway—they call it El Metro in Mexico City—pulls into the Piño Suarez station. People bustle to the steps that lead to the street, meander past the store windows of the shopping arcade or pause to stare at a massive stone cube. The cube is crowned by a carved circle of rock that imperiously commands attention in the clean-swept, silent plaza that constitutes the other half of the Piño Suarez stop.

The cloud-gray sculpture is the offertory of the curled snake. It was the blood-drenched altar of Quetzalcoatl, the Feathered Serpent, guardian deity of Tenochtitlán, capital of the Aztecs, whose martial magnificence dazzled the Spaniards when they encountered it early in the sixteenth century.

The conquest of the Americas by Spain centered on the

clashes of values and will between three pairs of antagonists. In South America, history pitted Francisco Pizarro, the tiny swineherd from Estremadura with the wiry body and the character of fine-honed steel, against Atahuallpa, the pampered and revered son of an Inca who had pushed an empire to its final limits but whose offspring forgot that the foundation of the empire was unity in the ruling family.

In Central America, the two men who symbolized their peoples and civilizations represented an even starker contrast. On the Spanish side was red-bearded, auburn-haired Pedro de Alvarado, handsome, dashing, vain, a conquistador par excellence in the grandeur of his ambition and the scope of his greed. Facing him in the final battle was the Quiché prince Tecun Uman, reared in the Maya traditions of responsibility and wisdom, whose faith was rooted in the harmony of the universe. Characteristically, the decisive encounter between those two found the conquistador on horseback, wielding a lance, the prince on foot, swinging a cudgel. In military terms, there was no contest. Maya legend holds that when Tecun Uman fell, an eagle soared into the sky. But the prince was dead, and the conquistador's boot ground deeply and permanently into the Maya realm.

In North America, the two men who wrote their names into history, literally in blood and fire, were Hernán Cortés, elegant courtier, wily politician, an unusual conquistador in the strains of sensitivity and conscience that often haunted his nights, but that never interfered with the unscrupulous activities of his days; and Montezuma, widely hated head of the rapacious Aztec empire, but personally a man of dignity, plagued by deep depression, whose nights were pampered by every privilege due an Aztec prince but whose days were bedeviled by misfortunes and crested by calamities that led to his death in chains and the collapse and ruin of the Aztec world.

Of the three encounters, the best known is the one between Montezuma and Cortés. In part because it was the first of the discoveries by Europeans of the great achievements that had been wrought in the Americas—a continent the Europeans initially thought to be the Indian subcontinent of Asia. That odd assumption was based on the characteristic narrowness of the European explorers' intent. Starting from their own continent and heading west, they wanted to find a new route to India and its riches of spices and sandalwood, emeralds and rubies. It never occurred to them that there might be anything but water between their domicile and their desire. When they first stumbled onto inhabited islands in the Caribbean, they were baffled. When they came upon the great civilizations of the American continent, they were at first incredulous, then awed and amazed. Their diaries and personal accounts, their letters home and missives to the court, are full of surprise and reluctant admiration. Both sentiments found an echo in Europe that has reverberated through the centuries.

The Cortés-Montezuma encounter has emerged as the most deeply edged of Europe's meetings with America's pre-Columbian civilizations also because it is the best documented. Cortés himself was a polished and perceptive writer and while his letters and reports suffer from self-serving distortions and the glossing over of his own and his comrades' more brutal machinations, he does offer a sweeping panorama of the civilizations he found. And one of his most steadfast captains, a solid, meticulous, no-nonsense soldier by name of Bernal Díaz, complemented Cortés's overview with a detailed, soundly observed account of his own that fills in most of the gaps left by Cortés's more elegant construction.

The third, and perhaps most compelling reason for the particular place the Cortés-Montezuma encounter holds in history is that it was in many ways an even match. The Mayas' glory transcended the conquistadors but they could not stand against the Spanish in battle or in politics. The Incas' great social achievements survived the Spaniards but

Inca society had no means of coping with conquistador guile. In the Aztecs the conquistadors had an adversary who was more than a match for them in courage and ruthlessness, in capacity for sacrifice, and in fanatic zeal.

Like the Spaniards in Europe, the Aztecs in the Americas were latecomers to power. Two centuries before the historic encounter, the Aztecs had been a nomadic tribe, wandering hungry around the semideserts of the north. They were brutal barbarians when they pushed south, detested and despised by the more settled and civilized communities they met in their migrations. To rid themselves of the Aztecs' obnoxious presence, one civilized community that did not want to engage in bloody battle with these barbarians, assigned to them a snake-infested island in the shallow lakes of the central plateau that is today the site of Mexico City. From that unlikely spot, the Aztecs managed, within a few decades, to build up an empire unprecedented in North America. To do this, they stopped at nothing—in their demands of themselves and their extortions from others. From themselves, they exacted iron discipline and a devotion, bordering on mania, to self-sacrifice. From others, they took, without qualm, whatever they needed or wanted: food and clothes; forced labor to build their causeways and houses; women to serve them in their homes and beds; and, above all, men, women and children to sacrifice in their temples and to provide their gods with "the precious liquid"—human blood—that the Aztecs believed was the only nourishment fit for the deities.

The Aztec pantheon had many denizens, all of them wrenching from man at least as much as they gave. Among the major gods, Tlaloc, the rain god, produced floods and hurled hail as easily as he offered the rich drops of moisture that made crops grow. In Aztec sculpture, Tlaloc looks cruel and mean, with a massive square face and deeply ringed eyes that give him the appearance of a rattlesnake. Coatlicue, the major female divinity, the earth mother, devours as fiercely as she nourishes. Her hands and feet are

For the Aztecs, the serpent was a symbol of the earthbound nature of man. The divine Feathered Serpent could also reach for the sky.

fangs and claws, her girdle is a snake and her necklace is made of human hearts and skulls. The Aztecs' tribal god, Huitzilopochtli, the god of fire, is a wizened, wicked-looking creature, who speaks more eloquently of flaring volcanoes that make the earth tremble than of the quiet glow that warms the hearth.

The only exception to this parade of divine terrors is Quetzalcoatl, the Feathered Serpent, who is part god, part man, with a long history of battling the jealous divinities in the service of mankind, but subject himself to the weaknesses and temptations that inevitably vanquish man and bring about his fall from power. Power, not grace. For the Aztecs, the two were synonymous. Quetzalcoatl, stern and rigid in expression, entangled in costume and weapons, heavily burdened by a gigantic headdress of feathers, was the most benign of the plethora of deities the Aztecs felt they had to placate. They believed that the serpent that was part of Quetzalcoatl's dual nature signified that man could never hope to stop groveling on the ground, but that, on the other hand, the plumes on Quetzalcoatl's head indicated that at least man's mind could attempt to fly. Quetzalcoatl, the Feathered Serpent, was as close as the Aztecs came to conceiving of duality in themselves or in nature. For the rest, their lives were full of contradictions that moved them from terror to depression, from blunt stoicism to a burning and often deadly fanaticism.

The society they built inevitably reflected this viewpoint and these values. It, too, was full of contradictions. The Aztecs had only the rudiments of a written language, but their poetry, composed in the mind, declaimed at court, and passed on in oral tradition, was lovely and very sad. They thought of poems as wreaths of flowers, exquisite, fragrant, fading, and subject to quick death. They thought of human life as having even less reality than that; of being not a life at all, but a short dreamlike journey through existence, barely tasted, hardly touched, and not understood. A famous Aztec poem about the life of man goes:

We have come only to sleep
We have come only to dream.
It is not true, it is not true
That we have come to live on the earth.

As at every spring the grass is renewed,
So do we too acquire form.
Our heart puts out shoots, grows green.
Our body begets a few flowers
And then lies withered.

Aztec society was tightly disciplined and infinitely demanding of its members, but the Aztecs also constructed the only pre-Columbian civilization that educated *all* its children, boys and girls, high-born or low, members of every class and occupation. No other society in the world at that time had a comparable system of schooling. Moreover, despite its cast-iron rigidities, Aztec society acknowledged individual merit and rewarded talent of any kind—military or artistic, scientific or priestly. It also appreciated and protected its merchants, who traveled far facing hazards and hardships, and its craftsmen, who labored hard, although there was little joy or inspiration in their work.

In most other societies in the world at that time, men and women were born to a caste and to a task to which they were bound for life. This was not true among the Aztecs. Any gifted boy could make his way through the rigors of the *calmecac,* the school for the talented, and emerge as an artist of the court or, even more desirable in the Aztec system, as a member of the elite corps of the Knights of the Jaguar or the Knights of the Eagle, whose presence was feared and prowess admired throughout the Aztec realm and, by reputation, beyond. Every Aztec girl could, by her beauty and accomplishments, aspire to high social status as wife, consort, or concubine to a prince or a knight. With arcane knowledge and curing skills, she could practice healing and magic, an occupation regarded with reverence and awe.

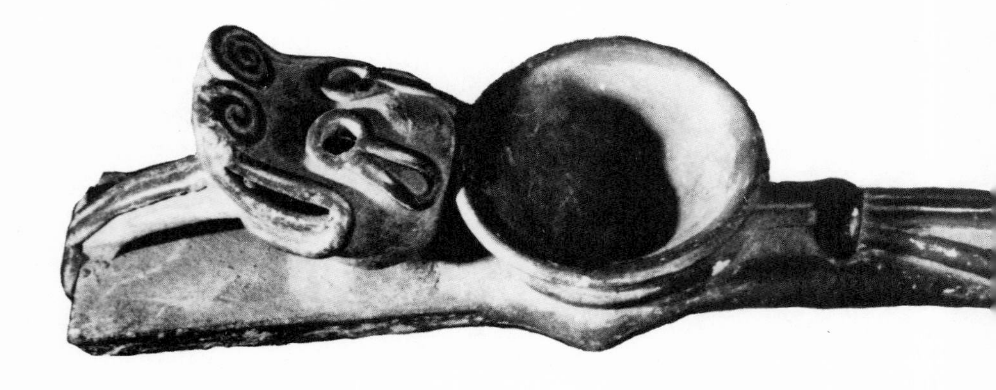

Notorious for the brutality and ruthlessness of their conquests, the Aztecs also conceived of "the war of flowers," the pre-Columbian equivalent to the joustings of King Arthur's knights. In these "flower wars," men who held no enmity in their hearts, or thoughts of territorial conquest in their minds, matched courage and military skill to test themselves, their character and their art. However, if a European knight was felled in a joust, he was mourned and buried; if an Aztec knight died, he was celebrated and his heart offered to the gods.

The Aztecs had no prisons, at least in the sense of walled fortresses or subterranean dungeons in which prisoners were kept, far away from the sympathy and solace of their fellow men. This was astonishing in a society that took literally thousands of prisoners each year and killed them. Aztec prisoners were kept in open cages in the streets and courtyards of cities, and people were encouraged to feed the captives and talk with them. In a way, the prisoners were honored guests, although the hospitality offered them

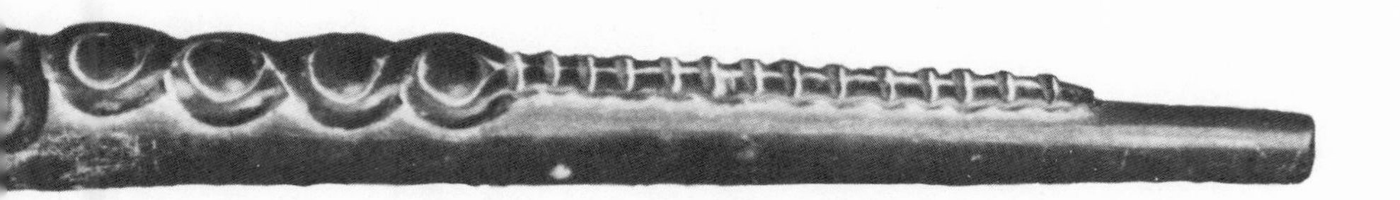

This is the kind of flute a princely prisoner played as he ascended the temple steps to be sacrificed.

tended to be brief. They were destined for death, but a death designed not for human revenge but for appeasement of the gods whose good will, won with the victims' blood and hearts, would redound to the benefit of all mankind.

The epitome of this attitude was the princely prisoner, a high caste volunteer, who had to be extremely handsome and who, for one full year, got the best Aztec society had to offer: lavish food and drink; feather mantles and jewelry; music and dance whenever he wanted; lovely women to serve him at all times. He was lodged in one of the Aztecs' beautiful gardens (gardens and arboreta became a specialty of the Aztecs when their civilization reached its height) but could wander about the city at will. On the day of his death, he was given a potent, well-spiced drink drugged with a sweet-smelling hallucinogen and crowned with a circlet of flowers. Playing a flute, he ascended the steps of the temple to the offertory at the top. There he stretched out languorously on the curved stone and priests slashed open his chest and lifted out the still beating heart, which they held high for the worshipers below to see. The crowd's moans at the sight were an expression of both gratitude and ecstasy.

When the Spaniards marched into Tenochtitlán in the autumn of 1519, Aztec civilization had come a long way from its beginnings on the snake-infested island. Whether it had reached its height we will never know, because the Spaniards imposed their own values on the Aztecs, thereby preventing any further growth. But what the Spaniards found was impressive enough. The empire was large, and rigidly run. Wealth poured into the Aztec cities in a steady stream, consisting of services as well as goods, skills and talents as well as the brawn of slaves and the bodies of sacrificial victims.

While the Maya enriched and inspired the people of all societies with whom they came into contact, and the Inca avidly incorporated the accomplishments of the peoples they absorbed into their realm, the Aztecs annexed whatever and whoever they fancied. Thus, the Aztec capital of Tenochtitlán was awash with Maya artists and scholars, Mixtec scribes and goldsmiths, Zapotec sculptors and painters. The famous "Aztec Calendar" was actually a barbarized version of the astronomical calculations of the ancient Olmecs with cataclysmic Aztec superstitions superimposed.

Nevertheless, the Aztecs' systematic rapacity produced interesting, many-faceted cities. White-washed palaces and houses gleamed under the highland sun. Smooth, raised causeways radiated into the island capital. Aqueducts brought fresh water into the city from springs in the hills; sewers removed the garbage; floating gardens in the lake dripped with flowers that decorated homes and produced colors for painting. Well-built bridges spanned the canals of the city and the waterways were thronged with people in sleek canoes going about their business, which was mainly to bring goods to the large, well-organized and richly stocked market of Tenochtitlán. Towering above the lively activities brooded squat, blood-drenched temples, often

The Olmecs' "mother culture" featured the jaguar as its basic symbol. Here an Olmec man emerges from a jaguar's jaw.

paired—one temple decorated with serpents dedicated to Tlaloc, the rain god; the other, festooned with skulls, to Huitzilopochtli, the god of fire.

Captain Bernal Díaz who, with Cortés, climbed the 114 steps of Tenochtitlán's main sanctuary the day the conquistadors entered the Aztec capital, describes the view from the top of the temple, noting first that in the offertories that faced the images of the gods to whom the temples were dedicated, "the walls were so crusted with blood and the floor was so bathed in it that in the slaughterhouses of Castile there was no such stink."

What Cortés and Captain Díaz saw was amazing:

"We could see all three of the causeways that led into Mexico. . . .

"We saw the fresh water that came from Chapultepec, which supplied the city, and the bridges on the three causeways, built at certain intervals so the water could go from one part of the lake to another, and a multitude of canoes, some arriving with provisions and others leaving with merchandise.

"We saw that every house in this great city and in the others built on the water could be reached only by wooden drawbridges or by canoe. We saw temples built like towers and fortresses in these cities all whitewashed; it was a sight to see."

It was not just the physical aspect of Aztec cities that astonished the conquistadors. They were surprised as well by the smooth functioning of Aztec society.

In Captain Díaz's words:

"After taking a good look and considering all that we had seen we looked again at the great square and the throngs of people, some buying, others selling. The buzzing of their voices could be heard more than a league away. There were soldiers among us who had been in many parts of the world, in Constantinople and Rome and all over Italy, who said that they had never before seen a market place so large and so well laid out and so filled with people."

CHAPTER TWO

Legacies and Acquisitions

WHAT gave rise to the Aztecs' cataclysmic vision of the universe is still a mystery. None of the civilizations that flourished in the areas that fell into the Aztec domain—and whose values and achievements the Aztecs adopted—felt quite the same way about the human condition.

The earliest of the civilizations we know of (even today's Mexicans speak of it as "the mother culture") was that of the Olmecs, which dates back to at least 1,000 B.C. We do not as yet know very much about Olmec beliefs but they seem to have been a people that prized serenity and were, generally speaking, thoughtful but content with their lot. Most early civilizations had a special identification with one animal—the Chinese with the dragon, the Assyrians with the bull, the Romans with the wolf. For the Olmecs,

An Olmec bowl. The animal in the foot of the bowl is a stylized jaguar, representing to the Olmecs both power and the sun.

the animal was the jaguar, which represented both power and the sun. When they wanted to suggest that a human being was particularly powerful, they gave him the features of a big, wild cat. According to one interesting theory, the five dots and the single dash that are the basic ingredients of the Olmecs' mathematical system derive from the imprint of the jaguar's paw, the dash being the mark left by the palm, the five dots reflecting the imprint of the claws.

The Olmecs also had a particular affinity with the duck. Theirs was a coastal civilization—the Olmec heartland was the coast of the Gulf of Mexico—and the duck probably represented to them water and therefore fertility. When they were not giving their supermen feline features, they decorated them with duck bills. In both cases, the results are startling, but appealing.

The entire Olmec civilization seems to have been that way: startling in its extraordinary achievements, appealing in its profound humanity.

The Olmecs, it seems, way back before the Greeks and the Romans, and even before the Persians and Medes, had a system of arithmetic, based on those jaguar paws; a written language, consisting of hieroglyphs (we have samples of these glyphs, but do not know what they say); a hydraulic system that included pools and drains; acrobatic accomplishments that seem close to impossible; a political system that apparently included a kind of town meeting, or at least a governing council that debated; and sculptural skills so superb that, 3,000 years later, they still inspire admiration and awe.

Indeed, what we know about the Olmecs we owe largely to their sculpture. The smaller pieces are carved in what is known as blue jade, which is really a blue-black kind of jade with an intense shimmer that looks almost like polished ebony. From this fortunately durable material, the Olmecs shaped their duck-billed and jaguar-featured symbols of power, their serene and meditative men and women, their chubby, laughing children, and their "yokes," a carved,

yoke-shaped belt that shows acrobats poised in postures that call to mind the fanciful leaps of the bull dancers of Crete who displayed, about five hundred years earlier, a similar kind of improbable excellence. Among the Olmecs, these stone belts were worn for a ball game that seems to have been played by almost all the pre-Columbian civilizations of North and Central America over a period of more than 2,500 years.

No Olmec architecture remains. They probably built with wood and wattle, materials that decay quickly in the hot and humid coast on the Gulf of Mexico. But they did leave us a form of architecture: massive heads carved of stone, as large as Egypt's sphinx and as challenging to the imagination. They set these heads down in the verdant, whispering jungles of their heartland and the expression on the rock faces changes with the light as it filters through the tropical foliage. The same kind of head—square, snub-nosed, with Mongoloid features—also appears on stelae, tall stone tablets, that are scattered through the Olmec heartland. One of these stelae shows what we assume to have been an Olmec flanked on one side by a person with the elegant features and elaborate headdress of an Egyptian, on the other by a man with clearly African features. On another stela, an Olmec is shown in conversation with a man sporting the curled beard and Semitic features of an Assyrian. Did the Olmecs have contact with Egypt, Africa, Assyria? We don't know, and may never find out. What we do know is that Olmec influence reached south to Panama and north to the borders of what today is the United States, and extended through all of Mexico from coast to coast, including the high central plateau where the Aztecs met it and fitted some of its features into their own civilization.

If the Olmecs were the "mother culture" of the Aztecs, the "father culture" was Teotihuacán. The Olmecs, in their hot and humid heartland, were imaginative and mysterious. The people of Teotihuacán, located on the cool plateau

Olmec sculpture was famous for its "smiling children." This one has Mongoloid features; others had African and Semitic features.

An Olmec woman. A happy person, she is typical of what seems to have been a serene civilization.

An Olmec child. More realistic than the stylized "smiling children" depicted in Olmec art, this youngster appears pretty content with life.

of Mexico's central valley with its bracing sparkling air, were logical and precise, with a sense of ordered proportion that can be seen in their temples and palaces and in the faces of their men and women. Evocative remnants of Teotihuacán exist just outside Mexico City, in a valley wedged between the western and eastern sierras. Facing each other in the valley are the tall temples of the Sun and the Moon with thirteen other sanctuaries placed geometrically between these two main temples. Three hundred and sixty-five figures decorate the sanctuaries. The causeways of Teotihuacán are perfectly parallel and the entire arrangement is imbued with a sense of symmetry that is not so much pleasing to the eye as soothing to the mind.

An Olmec "yoke," really a stone belt that was worn by players of the ritual ball game that was common to many pre-Columbian civilizations.

A typical —gigantic— Olmec face, with helmet. These sculpted stone heads eye visitors at the Olmec site of La Venta.

The faces of the people of Teotihuacán—they have come down to us in statues of stone and obsidian—exude the same spirit. Their features are not realistic, like those of the Olmecs. Teotihuacán faces are sketched in stone by a few simple lines that add up, nevertheless, to a recognizable expression of stern symmetry that echoes the atmosphere of the temple complex.

Teotihuacán palaces fit into the same spiritual scheme. Grouped around a quadrangle, they are themselves clean-lined oblongs with pillared terraces facing a central courtyard. The inner rooms are cool and softly lit through entranceways that face a terrace. The floors, ceilings, walls, and pillars of the terraces are covered with white stucco and the walls are painted in muted earth colors.

Teotihuacán was the first real city in the Americas: not just a ceremonial center to which people came to worship on festive occasions, but a permanent place of residence for the tens of thousands, perhaps even hundreds of thousands, who lived and worked there.

The Teotihuacán civilization began to shape itself during the first two or three centuries of the Christian era, achieved its greatest glory during the "classical period" between A.D. 300 and 900, then crumbled quickly, in the span of a few years. While it lasted, its influence spread widely, although not quite as far as that of the Olmecs. But it left important memories. Subsequent generations came to think of the people of Teotihuacán as a race of giants. Perhaps this happened because the bones of large animals were found there and were wrongly thought to be human in origin. Or perhaps the legend of the giants of Teotihuacán arose because the temples of Teotihuacán are so vast in scale—the base of the temple of the sun is larger than that of the pyramid near Cairo. Teotihuacán also remained in the imagination of subsequent generations as "the place of the gods," which is what the word Teotihuacán means. Myths began to develop, tales of the gods meeting in Teotihuacán, consulting and quarreling there, and deciding,

A child and a man of Teotihuacán, the "father culture" of the Aztecs. Ruins of Teotihuacán can still be seen just outside of Mexico City.

in their own dramatic way, to create the sun and the moon, the stars and man. Teotihuacán became to the people who lived in pre-Columbian Mexico what Mount Olympus was to the Greeks.

To the Aztecs, Teotihuacán left a particular legacy. In Teotihuacán we see for the first time the snake-bird-god, the famous Feathered Serpent that became such a vital ingredient in the religious faith of the Aztecs. It stood for the image they had of themselves which, in turn, inspired both their rapid rise to power and the superstitious speculation that contributed so to their fall.

While Teotihuacán flourished in the cool valley between the sierras, a softer, gentler "sister culture" matured in the warmer climes of the south. That was the civilization of the Maya, centered in the south of Mexico and in what today are the countries of Guatemala and Honduras. The Maya's classical age parallels that of Teotihuacán. Like Teotihuacán, the Maya realm was a theocracy, governed by rulers who were priests. The cement that held both realms together was not so much power, but a shared sense of values, not military might but religious and spiritual conviction. Unlike the people of Teotihuacán, however, the Maya were artists and scientists who seem to have inherited from the Olmecs such cultural phenomena as the erection of stelae, decorated with carvings and the glyphs of a written but still undeciphered language; a ball game that had deep religious significance; and a passion for sculpture, which the Maya developed to a height that has earned them the designation "the Greeks of the Americas." The Maya also painted exquisitely: murals like the one discovered in a temple at Bonampak, in the southern Mexican state of Chiapas, and illustrations of books, only three of which escaped the holocaust of the conquistadors' book-burning.

Like the people of Teotihuacán, the Maya were also great architects, although Maya architecture was both more sensitive and more sophisticated than that of Teotihuacán. The Maya invented the arch—a corbelled vault—that lent a

The Feathered Serpent as depicted by the people of Teotihuacán.

grace to their building unmatched by any other pre-Columbian civilization. Maya temples were as tall as those of Teotihuacán, but where the atmosphere generated by Teotihuacán was impressive, Maya sites were exquisite. In the Maya realm, the stern symmetry of Teotihuacán is replaced with a rich harmony, which was reflected as well in the Maya's beliefs and way of life.

The Aztecs absorbed little of the Maya's grace or philosophy. But when the Aztecs had reached the height of their power, and wanted to add the solace of luxury to the rigors of prowess, they brought to their capital of Tenochtitlán, by persuasion or force, some of the artists from the Maya realm. The Maya civilization, like that of Teotihuacán, had crumbled by then and Maya art had decayed. But even in its degraded state, Maya art was infinitely superior to the crude concepts and clumsy crafts the Aztecs had acquired in their single-minded concentration on conquest.

The civilization with which the Aztecs identified most closely and easily was that of the Toltecs, who ruled Mexico's central valley for about three hundred years after Teotihuacán fell.

Prowling, and later pushing their way south from their homeland in the northern desert, the barbaric Toltecs brought with them an array of concepts and inventions the Aztecs adopted. One of these inventions was a new weapon, the spear thrower, a contraption that made it possible to hurl a spear over a considerable distance, thus considerably enlarging a warrior's aggressive range.

Another Toltec accomplishment that the Aztecs imitated was their form of military organization. The Toltecs had established the first military orders in the Americas, a social caste with special obligations and privileges. Unlike other pre-Columbian societies, whose young men fought when there was a war but otherwise dedicated themselves to normal peacetime pursuits, the Toltecs had military or-

A scene from the paradise of Tlaloc, the rain god.
It is part of a mural in a restored palace near Teotihuacán.

ders made up of full-time warriors, whose martial careers began in the late teens with rigorous training and usually ended in death. The Toltecs had two military orders: the Order of the Jaguar and the Order of the Coyote. The Aztecs took over the concept and structure of the orders but changed the name of one of the knighthoods. They retained the Knights of the Jaguar, but converted the military Order of the Coyote—a name that perhaps reminded them too insistently of their own wild and hungry desert days—to the Knights of the Eagle. The eagle has a vital place in Aztec legend and served as their symbol of soaring glory, not unlike the role the eagle plays in the national imagery of the United States.

The Toltecs also brought with them from their northern desert their view of the universe as violent and terror-filled—a view adopted by the Aztecs, and one which made Aztec lives so stormy and sad. The Toltecs believed that the world had already been created five times, and that each of the previous creations had collapsed in blood and thunder. They thought of their own age as "the fifth sun," a sun that had to be nourished by "the precious liquid," human blood. The Toltecs launched the grim practice of human sacrifice on a major scale, including the mystical act of cutting out the living heart of the sacrificial victim and offering it to the sun in supplication for continued warmth and light.

The Toltecs also made one major nonmurderous contribution to Aztec civilization: the cult of the Feathered Serpent, Quetzalcoatl. In Toltec mythology the Feathered Serpent represented the capacity of man to soar to the sky as well as crawl on the ground, his ability to somehow combine in his mind and nature the two polarities of heaven and earth. Among the Toltecs there was also a historical person called Quetzalcoatl, who became a legendary hero, comparable in some ways to King Arthur and his knights of the round table in the Kingdom of Camelot.

In Toltec tales, the man Quetzalcoatl represents, like Arthur and his knights, a better way of life. Toltec legend says that Quetzalcoatl came to teach the Toltecs new crafts and skills. Having instructed the Toltec people, he left, walking east until he disappeared in the ocean. But he vouchsafed a promise to return at a later age. When the Spaniards arrived on the east coast of the Aztec realm, with animals and weapons the Aztecs had never seen, it was easy for the Aztecs to believe that Cortés was Quetzalcoatl, who had returned as promised. Montezuma himself held that belief until watching Cortés in action convinced him otherwise. By then it was too late.

The Toltecs established a capital at Tula, as close to today's Mexico City as Teotihuacán but in another direction. The ruins of Tula remain: a complex of temples grouped around a central square and, in the heart of the square, the ubiquitous Toltec altar bluntly designed for human sacrifice. Tula's main temple was supported by giant columns hewed as Toltec warriors in full regalia, each with an enormous spear thrower at his side, a butterfly breastplate on his chest, feathers on his sandaled feet, a feather diadem on his head. In the back, a sun god emerges from a flower that serves as a kind of belt buckle. The sun god does not smile. The warrior pillars, too, look grim. From their temple height they stare at the square of sacrifice where the Toltecs' special contribution to pre-Columbian sculpture, the *chac mol,* curves in supine stupor. The chac mol is a stone figure, with a bland, apathetic face, its lap broadened and curved to hold the human body arched back to offer its chest to the flint knife of the priest. The chac mol, too, is a Toltec legacy the Aztecs acquired with appreciation.

The Toltec civilization, in fact, so suited the Aztecs' own inclinations and aims that, when the Aztecs had made their own bloody way to empire, they felt the need for an aristocratic lineage and chose the Toltecs as their ancestors. The choice was pure invention. The only real origin the two civilizations had in common was that they both originally infiltrated, as nomad barbarians from the north, the already civilized Central Valley of Mexico.

A stone frieze of Quetzalcoatl, the Feathered Serpent, and Tlaloc, the rain god.

Two additional civilizations contributed a selection of their accomplishments to the Aztec realm. To incorporate what these civilizations had to offer, the Aztecs had to reach south to the Oaxaca Valley, another plateau set in the mountain chains of Mexico, but warmer and lovelier than the Central Valley that nourished Teotihuacán, the Toltecs, and the Aztecs.

The Oaxaca Valley was home to the Zapotecs and the Mixtecs. The Zapotecs were the earlier and longer-lasting of the two societies. The many-layered Zapotec civilization shows influences from Toltec, Teotihuacán, Maya, and even Olmec sources. The two great extant Mixtec and Zapotec sites are Mitla and Monte Albán, both in the Oaxaca Valley, with Monte Albán a veritable layer cake of Zapotec history and Mitla an enchanting sample of the Mixtecs' delicate and delightful sense of decoration.

There are really four Monte Albáns, all located on the commanding heights of a series of hills overlooking the Oaxaca Valley. They date from about 500 B.C. to around A.D. 1000. The later Monte Albáns display such accomplishments as a well-designed observatory and sun dial, and priests' apartments that have an underground passage leading to the central altar of a temple compound. The speculation is that the reigning priest—the Zapotecs' political system was also a theocracy—appeared before the awed eyes of the multitudes as if out of nowhere, from the center of the earth, to utter his predictions of their fate for the season or the year. The oracle at Delphi, in ancient Greece, worked on a similar principle.

The earlier Monte Albáns hold puzzles. There is, for example, a series of tomb carvings depicting "dancers," human bodies in various, rather improbable motions, with facial features that span a range of races. The faces look Egyptian, black African, Semitic, Mongoloid and Olmec. The puzzle is, where did these facial notions come from? Was there contact at some time between Africa, Asia, and the people of this remote valley in the heart of Mexico?

Another question posed at Monte Albán derives from "the medical school," another series of rock carvings that show, quite accurately, a series of biological phenomena including a kind of X-ray view of a woman giving birth to a baby. How much medical knowledge did the Zapotecs have, and where did it come from? We do not know. But we do know that the Zapotecs' skills in decorative design, which they displayed in their public buildings and their homes as well as in their costumes and their jewelry, were absorbed by the Aztecs during their "luxury period." The way the Aztecs did this was by commanding Zapotec craftsmen to practice their skills in Aztec cities.

The Zapotecs first met the Aztecs when the Zapotecs made the mistake of asking for Aztec protection against the Mixtecs, their sister civilization in the Oaxaca Valley.

The Mixtecs were originally a mountain people who had come late to the valley and seemed poised to take it over. To prevent this, the Zapotecs asked the Aztecs for help. The Aztecs responded promptly in their fashion, by establishing hegemony over the entire valley.

The contribution the Mixtecs made to the Aztec empire was literacy. The Mixtecs were compilers of books—like the Maya they painted glyphs and illustrations on deerskin or treated tree bark—and at least three of the Mixtecs' books have survived. They are now called codices and long journeys have landed them far away from the Oaxaca Valley in which they were written. One of the Mixtec codices is now in the Vatican in Rome; another is in the library of the French Chamber of Deputies in Paris; a third is in Harvard University's Peabody Museum in Cambridge, Massachusetts.

The Aztecs used the Mixtecs as their scribes. They also used Mixtec woodcarvers, goldsmiths, and jewelers. The Mixtecs worked metal into delicate filigree and composed mosaic patterns in turquoise. The Aztecs loved the Mixtecs' delicate creations. They acquired the Mixtec genius in the classic Aztec way: by collecting the creations them-

A gold mask from Monte Albán, the work of craftmen of the Zapotec civilization.

selves as tribute, or by ordering the people who produced them to live and labor in Tenochtitlán.

One more important cultural group preceded the arrival of the Aztecs in the central valley, but theirs was a civilization the Aztecs tried to ignore. They were the Chichimecs whose name means "line of dogs." The connotation is not a purely pejorative one. In most pre-Columbian civilizations, dogs were bred as a delicacy, and eaten much like suckling pigs are today. The flavor is said to have been comparable. Still, the inference is one of weakness and of a low animal nature, although the most advanced of the Chichimec principalities (there were many in the fourteenth and fifteenth centuries) achieved a fairly high state of civilization. Some Chichimecs made extended trips to the Oaxaca Valley, acquired some of the Mixtec skills, and brought these back to their own cities. The greatest of the Chichimec princes was the poet-king Nezahualcoyotl, who reigned late in the fifteenth century, wrote lovely, thoughtful verses and brought artists and philosophers to his court. Nezahualcoyotl was held in high esteem throughout the Central Valley of Mexico. Even his Aztec contemporaries admired him and established an intimate relationship with him. In the Aztec style, it was a patchwork of alliances and betrayals.

But Nezahualcoyotl was an exception as far as the Aztecs were concerned. As a general rule, the Aztecs considered themselves greatly superior to the Chichimecs. In historic fact they were, like the Chichimecs, barbarian invaders, and latecomers to the Central Valley that had seen great civilizations rise and fall for a thousand years before the first Aztec ever set foot on the plateau.

CHAPTER THREE

The Crane People

AZTEC legend concedes that the Aztec people emerged into the world from a cave in the northwest. The cave was situated on an island in a lake, and was surrounded by tall rushes in which birds with long legs and pointed beaks kept alive by hunting in the water for their sustenance. The name of the island was Aztatlan, which means "the place of the cranes." In their early days the Aztecs thought of themselves as "The Crane People," and the image left them with two character traits they were unable to shed. These traits are an embarrassed consciousness of their primitive origins and a deep nostalgia for those sad and silent days when all they knew was the gentle lapping of water against the island, the rushes singing in the wind, and the tall cranes diving for food amid the weeds or spreading their white-gray wings for short flights to another island.

The Aztecs went to great lengths to overcome their origins. Their first effort was to create for themselves a tribal deity to inspire, advise, and lead them as they struck out from their island caves into the unknown that lay south and west. Aztec legend holds that in their migrations the crane people were led by four priests, and the first carried on his shoulders the image of the Aztec god, Huitzilopochtli. The word means "hummingbird on the left." Searching for hummingbirds on the left would indeed have brought the wandering crane people southeast, to what is today the Valley of Mexico, where the crane people's years of migration ended. How the lovely hummingbird on the left became the ferocious god of fire that dominated Aztec theology and the Aztec way of life is a depressing question, still unanswered.

But the metamorphosis began early, apparently when the Aztecs first reached Tula, the capital of the militaristic Toltecs, whom they adopted as a model for their own civilization. Aztec legend tells of a virtuous widow who lived in Tula and who, while sweeping the temple one day as an act of piety, found a ball of feathers on the temple grounds which she tucked away between her breasts. The consecrated feathers are the Aztec version of the Christian symbolism of the Annunciation, and the virtuous lady of Tula found herself pregnant a few months later. Unlike Mary, however, the widow was not a virgin but already had a daughter and "400" (i.e., innumerable) sons. These children got angry at what they considered their widowed mother's unpardonable transgression and decided to kill her. The sons armed themselves and marched on the temple their mother served. As they approached, the widow heard a voice within her saying, "Don't be frightened; I will protect you." Within seconds, the voice embodied itself into a fully armed warrior who materialized, adult and ready for combat, in a manner comparable to the Greeks' Athena who also sprang, fully equipped for war, from the brow of her father, Zeus.

The miraculous warrior emerging from the lady of Tula was Huitzilopochtli, and his arsenal consisted not only of

the traditional Toltec sword and *atlatl* (spear-thrower) but included a new, divine weapon: the serpent of fire that leaped in a hissing arc of flame to kill, with efficiency and dispatch, everyone of the "400" sons and their sister.

Aztec theology elevated this rather cruel tale by explaining that the widow was really mother earth, the daughter the moon, the sons the stars, and Huitzilopochtli the sun which must, each day, overcome the moon and the stars to make it possible for mankind to live. This imposed on Huitzilopochtli's people a special obligation. Since he was the sun, they were the people of the sun, whose glorious duty it was to see to it that the sun always received the nourishment it required. In Aztec belief that nourishment was the most precious gift mankind could offer: human blood.

Later in the development of their civilization, when the Aztecs encountered the more serene and advanced values of Teotihuacán, with its own image of the Feathered Serpent, they refined their ideas. The serpent of fire could warm as well as destroy; and the Feathered Serpent could fly and know both the earth on which it slithered and the heavens to which it could soar.

One additional legend is important in Aztec mythology. Having wandered for many years under the guidance of Huitzilopochtli, the Aztecs finally felt a need to settle. But Huitzilopochtli warned them that they could not do so until they came to an island on which they would encounter an eagle perched on a cactus holding a snake in its beak. They came upon that fateful eagle on a marshy clump of land, covered with reeds and rushes, in the Lake of Texcoco.

The Mexicayotl Chronicle, one of the Mexican "histories" that were written after the conquest in Nahuatl, the Aztec language, phonetically reproduced in the Spanish alphabet, retells the legend.

"Then Huitzilopochtli spoke again: 'Hear me, for there is something else that you have not yet seen. Go at once to see *tenoch,* on which you will see an eagle happily nesting, sunning himself there, and you should be pleased, for this is where the heart of *copil* was born. We shall find ourselves equipped with arrow and shield, and conquer and seize all those who surround us, for here will be our Mexican homeland, the place where the eagle screams and spreads his wings and eats, the place where the fish swims, the place where the serpent is torn apart and many things will happen.'

"And when they arrived at the place, they saw the eagle perched upon the *nopal,* happily eating and tearing apart his food and as soon as the eagle saw them he lowered his head. Although they saw him from very far, they saw that his nest was made of various precious feathers, and saw the heads of all kinds of birds scattered about. And at once the people wept because of this and said: 'We are rewarded; we have attained our desire since we have seen and marveled at the place where our new settlement will be. Let us go there and rest.' "

In the course of their wanderings, the Aztecs had also conceived of a nephew of their all-powerful Huitzilopochtli, who interpreted and edited the words of his uncle, filling a role similar to Moses, who took the people of Israel to their promised land. To the Aztecs, "setting eyes on the place where the heart of *copil* was born," signified that they had arrived in the long-promised land.

Tenoch and *nopal* are both Nahuatl words for cactus. To this day, Mexicans make a delicious salad out of cactus leaves cut into little pieces and marinated. The cactus leaves are called *nopalitas.*

The word *tenoch* was preserved in Tenochtitlán, the capital of the Aztec empire. Tenochtitlán means "the place of the cactus," a place that grew in size, solidity, and splendor to become the magnificent city that so impressed the Spaniards less than two centuries after its founding. And that legendary eagle on the cactus is still the central emblem of Mexico's coat of arms.

But how did the Aztecs, the crane people from the remote caves of the northwestern frontier, become "Mexicans," which means the people of the center, the core nation? It seems that after the Aztecs encountered the Toltec civilization at Tula, they not only invented themselves an unconquerable deity, they also concocted a historic lineage. Later, they were to claim Toltec descent. But when they first arrived in Toltec territory this was not possible; so they conceived of something more mysterious and, in a sense, even more presumptuous. They were "Mexicas," people of the center. At first, when others asked, "center of what?" they answered, "of the moon." Later, other people no longer dared to ask. And finally it became only too evident: They were the central power from coast to coast, from the empty desert of the north to the rampant jungles of the south.

The Aztecs enter history—and the Valley of Mexico—early in the thirteenth century. They arrived in the valley in 1215 and, at first, brought with them the primitiveness and vagrant habits characteristic of their wandering ways, plus the blood-thirsty, belligerent morals and mores they had designed for themselves as Huitzilopochtli's "people of the sun." This combination of traits made them extremely unpopular with all the peoples that had settled in the valley earlier and every community that encountered them wanted only to get rid of them as quickly as possible.

The Aztec way of proceeding was to stay a year or more at a place they had chosen, without much regard for others who might have had an earlier or ongoing claim, and in that place to set up sanctuary for Huitzilopochtli. The sanctuary was a combination of sacrificial altar and oracle. They sacrificed whatever living thing they could lay their hands on to feed Huitzilopochtli with the blood he desired—although in those early days they stopped short of human sacrifice—and he in turn advised them on where to go and how to get there. Obeying his instructions, they sent out scout-pioneers in the direction he advised, who went ahead to the site and planted a crop, which would then be ready for harvest when the rest of the tribe arrived.

After some sixty years of this "search-and-plant" procedure, the Aztecs came to the lovely, and strategically placed, "Hill of the Grasshopper," Chapultepec, today the central park of Mexico City. There they settled down for a generation and absorbed some of the knowledge and civilization of the people around them. Their first "books" date from that period—folded fans of parchment made from the maguey plant and covered with simple pictures that tell the story of Aztec migrations and describe their early way of life. At that point, the Aztecs also adopted a calendar from their more advanced neighbors, which made it possible for them to institute periodic festivals geared to the cycle of the seasons. The calendar also improved agricultural skills. They learned to make and cultivate *chinampas,* the famous floating gardens that later impressed and delighted the Spaniards and please visitors to Mexico City to this day.

When the Aztecs settled on Chapultepec, all of what today is Mexico City was a shallow lake with numerous islands, large and small, and extensive areas of marshland. Some of the smaller islands were planted, first with cereals and later with flowers, looking verdant and brilliant on the pale green surface of the lake. More ingenious still, some of the earlier settlers in the valley had devised a way of filling in earth between the reeds of the marshland and doing this in a way that made the reeds serve as anchors, supporting and steadying a floating island. On these rich, moist spots of land they planted crops. Thus the Aztecs watched, learned, and later applied the knowledge with the systematic energy and aggressive grandeur that characterized so many of their efforts.

But even when the Aztecs had settled on Grasshopper Hill, they did not shed their obnoxious habits of rudeness, thievery, woman-stealing, and total disregard of other people's rights and feelings. Once again, the Aztecs managed to make themselves so objectionable that the people among whom they had settled, the Tepanecs and the Calhuacans, who were direct descendants of the great civilization of Teotihuacán, decided they had to get rid of these impossible strangers. The Tepanecs and Calhuacans banded together and, already aware of the Aztecs' militaristic qualities, devised a ruse to lure the men out of their fortifications on Grasshopper Hill. Then one segment of the combined Tepanec-Calhuacan force decimated the women and children who had been left behind, while another segment tackled the men. It was a rout the Aztecs never forgot.

Had the Aztecs been in the place of the Tepanecs and Calhuacans, they probably would have exterminated their enemies. The Calhuacans were more civilized. They assigned to the vanquished Aztecs a piece of land in a place called Tizapan, which was known for the snakes that infested it. Probably the Calhuacans hoped that the snakes would finish the job they had begun. But they had counted without Aztec perversity and ingenuity. By origin an island people, and accustomed during their long time of wandering to making use of everything that came their way, the Aztecs were delighted with the snakes. A chronicle of the period says: "The Mexicans rejoiced greatly as soon as they saw the snakes and they roasted and cooked them all and ate them all up." It was not what the Calhuacans had had in mind.

However delighted the Aztecs were by their feast of snakes, they did not intend to remain on a piece of land to which they had been assigned. Nor were they prepared to accept defeat at the hands of the Calhuacans, or anyone else.

Aztec strategy at that time was always formulated by their fierce and fiery deity. And, according to the Mexicayotl Chronicle, this is what Huitzilopochtli said: "Hear me. We will not remain here but go where we shall find those whom we shall capture and dominate. But we will not make the mistake of being nice to the Calhuacans. We will begin a war."

They did begin a war, and were defeated once again and expelled from Tizapán, this time with no place to go except into the wild marshland of the lake. As an Aztec poet put it later on:

The Mexicans who escaped from enemy hands
The old ones
Waded to the center of the water
Where the bullrush and the reeds were whispering.

There, in the aquatic wilderness that suited both their origins and their character, they laid the foundations of Tenochtitlán, their capital city, and of their empire. The date was 1325.

The Aztec marsh was surrounded by three established, powerful kingdoms, a fact which the Aztecs, given their turn of mind, perceived as a threat. They responded with the tactic they continued to use for the next two hundred years: they schemed and intrigued to play one against the other, paying when necessary the price of both indignity and death. At one point, for example, they allied themselves with their former enemies the Tepanecs, who demanded from them such absurd tribute as ducks from the lagoon that would lay their eggs at the precise moment they were delivered to the Tepanec overlords. The Aztecs complied.

The Aztecs also hired themselves out as mercenaries. They died by the thousands in the service of other chieftains, just to maintain among their neighbors the balance of terror which made the Aztecs feel secure.

At the same time, they worked frantically, fanatically, to turn their marshland territory into the kind of place that could become the heart of an empire. They planted chinampas; they gathered fish, shrimp, and other lake products which they traded for wood and stone, and they used the wood and stone to build, first a sanctuary for their ever-demanding god, and then the beginnings of palaces, houses, causeways, and markets.

By 1372, they felt established and important enough to decide they should become a kingdom. In choosing their king, they did not turn to the priests who had been their leaders until that time. They made the choice a power play of such shrewd, cold-blooded calculation that it appears awesome for the time—or for any time. They asked the Calhuacans, who had defeated them, sent them to the snake land, and defeated them again, to give them a member of the Calhuacan royal family to reign over them. The motive behind this strange gesture was that the Calhuacans were the descendants of the Toltecs and the Aztecs intended to claim for themselves lineal descent from that martial civilization. They would use it later to support their claim to superiority by ancestry as well as prowess. The name of that first Aztec king of Toltec descent was Acamapichtli.

Following Acamapichtli were two kings who tied the Aztecs closer to other, older kingdoms in the valley. The first was Huitzilihuitl, who married the daughter of the Lord of Cuernavaca. There is a tale of how the Mexican prince fell in love with the Cuernavacan princess whose father, a medicine man and magician, did not like the groom from Tenochtitlán and devised magic ways of frustrating the marriage. But he failed. There is also a theory that what drew Huitzilihuitl to Cuernavaca was not so much the charm of the princess, but the rich cotton fields to which the Aztecs would get access through this alliance.

The Aztecs' third king, Chimalpopoca, contracted an even more advantageous alliance. Chimalpopoca was the grandson of Tezozomoc, a wily and unscrupulous Tepanec tyrant, whose reign lasted an incredible sixty-three years. During this time he pulled together the motley fiefs and kingdoms of the entire Valley of Mexico and, through a network of alliances, a number of neighboring valleys as well. As it turned out, he built the base of the Aztec Empire. A Mexican historian says: "The Aztecs learned their lessons in the school of Tezozomoc."

The first to translate these lessons into action was the Aztecs' fourth king, Itzcoatl, who ascended the throne in 1427. He devised a triple alliance that defeated the Tepanecs and annexed their empire. At first the spoils were divided equally among the three partners, but in less than a decade the Aztecs had become the leading force in the alliance, using their military prowess as well as their claim to Toltec lineage to snatch their place at the top.

To strengthen the Aztec claim to Toltec ancestry, Itzcoatl took an action that, throughout the history of mankind, has been the harbinger of mindless violence. He ordered the burning of all books. Existing books, of course, told the true story of the Aztecs' origin and their very recent and inferior standing in the valley. Itzcoatl wanted to make certain that the facts of history did not interfere with the Aztecs' ambition.

The flare of that consuming ambition was brandished high and wide by Itzcoatl's successor, Montezuma I. With one of those ironies that history sometimes offers, Montezuma I was the most important architect of the empire that crashed under Montezuma II. The first Montezuma unleashed the campaigns of terror and treachery that resulted in subjecting to Aztec rule most of the far-flung empire the Spaniards encountered. The famous Mexican historian and anthropologist, Ignacio Bernal, sums up the campaigns of Montezuma I:

"Like an avalanche, the Aztec troops fell upon the peoples, broke down their resistance through surprise attacks, captured their chief if that was possible, mounted the temple and burned it. This was their signal of victory and thereafter was left only the work of dividing the booty, women, and prisoners, establishing a government submissive to Tenochtitlán, fixing the tribute and marching off to a new conquest."

Montezuma I also initiated the most revolting aspect of Aztec conquest, the sacrifice, by the thousands, of captured prisoners in order to offer their blood to Huitzilopochtli, the old tribal deity whom the Aztecs had turned into the sun god. That, too, was a device of devilish genius. No one could disagree with the idea that the sun was necessary and had to be nourished. If human blood was the nourishment required, as the Aztecs preached, then human beings had to be sacrificed for the purpose. That the human sacrifices were overwhelmingly non-Aztec was a political bonus the Aztecs appreciated—and kept quiet about.

Montezuma I also exhibited to perfection the other major trait in the Aztecs' dual personality. He was a builder, sculptor, town-planner, and a lover of flowers. During his reign, Tenochtitlán was transformed from a town in the marshland to a city of stone, resplendent with towering temples, massive sculptures, and exquisite gardens.

When Montezuma I died, in 1469, his successor Axayacatl carried on the tradition of never-ending conquest and destruction and equally fanatic construction and embellishment. One of the many places Axayacatl conquered was Tlatelolco, where five hundred years later U.S. Secretary of State Henry Kissinger met with his Latin American counterparts to formulate "The Declaration of Tlatelolco," calling for a new form of cooperation in the Americas. And we owe to Axayacatl the magnificent sculpture known as "the Aztec calendar," a votive stone which honors the sun and depicts Aztec myths of the sun's creation.

Two additional monarchs complete the dynastic chain to Montezuma II: Axayacatl's successor, Tizoc, reigned for only five years but made those five years count in conquests. That half decade has come down to us in the form of a mammoth sculpture known as "the stone of Tizoc," which depicts the king's apparently endless chain of victories. On that sculpture, Tizoc appears in the dress of

Huitzilopochtli, demonstrating the unrelenting hold that demonic deity had on the Aztec imagination.

Tizoc was succeeded by his brother Ahuizotl, who built an aqueduct for Tenochtitlán, completed Tenochtitlán's great double-altar temple and unleashed such a reign of blood-drenched terror that even in today's Mexico his name is still synonymous with dread. To dedicate the temple of Tenochtitlán he reputedly sacrificed 80,000 victims. What horrors he must have inflicted to obtain that number of prisoners haunts the imagination.

But he died ignominiously. In 1502, a broken dike caused a flood in Tenochtitlán and Ahuizotl, trying to escape the rising waters in his palace, smashed his head against the wooden lintel of a doorway. The concussion killed him.

Montezuma II, who succeeded Ahuizotl that year, was a very different man. He was a mystic, devoted to religious ritual, deeply superstitious to the point of believing that he was himself at least semidivine. No one was allowed to look at him, or touch him. Even the greatest nobles of the court had to approach him barefoot with eyes lowered, and before they could address him they had to perform a series of genuflections accompanied by what was almost an incantation: "Lord, my Lord, my Great Lord." Only then could they state the business that had brought them.

During Montezuma's reign, Aztec conquests continued, although the Aztecs were occupied increasingly with campaigns to crush rebellions by people unwilling or unable to put up any longer with Aztec tyranny. Montezuma himself paid scant attention to military matters. Surrounded by pomp and splendor he isolated himself in his palace, a court that was the epitome of sumptuous despotism.

In 1519, when the Spaniards landed in Mexico, Montezuma's empire encompassed eleven million people, an enormous number at that period of history. Tenochtitlán itself had 250,000 inhabitants, five times the population of London, England, that year.

CHAPTER FOUR

Singing the Pictures of the Book

BY the standards of their time, and *any* place, the Aztecs led a demanding but not a deprived existence. They lived in houses built of either adobe or stone, well constructed to protect them from rain, cold, or heat. Often the houses were whitewashed and painted, especially in the cities. Each house usually had a separate kitchen and a *temazcalli,* the Aztec version of the sauna, which they used at least once a day. While generally sparsely furnished, the houses held all the necessities of life in addition to some attractive amenities such as finely woven mats and shiny lacquer trays, along with well-shaped and often handsomely painted vases and bowls, plates and cups, jars, jugs, bowls and pitchers, boxes, and the famous big round-bellied *ollas* used to this day in Mexico to store water, berry juice, corn beer, or the most delicious drink of them all, the rich, brown, foam-topped *xocoatl* (chocolate).

The Europeans who came to the Americas encountered some forty cultivated agricultural products they had not known before. These included chocolate, tomatoes (*xictomatl* to the Aztecs), tobacco, corn in a variety of uses (grain, gruel, bread, and beer), and the miraculous maguey plant. The maguey looks like a large cactus candelabra and supplied fruit, salad, and an alcoholic beverage for the Aztecs' table as well as thread for garments, needles for sewing, and, along the axis of the plant's broad, hard spines, a place to nest for the white insect that produces cochineal, the vivid pigment known as Aztec red. And nibbling at the maguey plant's roots were fat, inch-long worms which, salted and fried, constituted one of the delicacies of the Mexican cuisine then, and do so now.

The Aztecs' diet was varied and nutritious. For meat, they had deer and rabbit, peccary and opossum, hare, turkey, chicken, a special kind of hairless dog and, one observant conquistador reports, fifty kinds of geese, duck and quail, which they domesticated and raised in their aquatic backyards. From the lake came fish and a wide variety of seafood such as snails and turtles, crabs and crawfish. Their staples were corn and beans, but their vegetables also included squash and pumpkin, calabash and onion, tomatoes, potatoes and yams, sweet arrowroot, avocado, and eggplant. A bowl of fruit in a well-stocked Aztec home could consist of apples and plums, cherries and papaya, several kinds of berries, pineapple, and an assortment of fruit with hard rinds and juicy insides that had rich names like *chirimoya* and *tejocote* and are consumed with pleasure by people throughout Mesoamerica to this day. The same home could also offer a plate of nuts that would have included popcorn exactly as we know it today, peanuts, and salted sunflower seeds nowadays called *pepitas* and served at the cocktail hour. Cocktail hour in the Aztec realm would have called for *chicha,* beer brewed of corn, or *pulque,* the fermented juice of the multi-purpose maguey plant, which was highly potent. But alcohol consumption was strictly regulated

For the Aztecs — as for all their predecessor civilizations — corn was a staple, and a deity. This is a corn god, holding ears of maize.

among the Aztecs, reserved essentially for religious purposes and for the old, who needed it, the Aztecs thought, to "heat up their blood."

Aztec cuisine was sophisticated as well as varied. The Aztecs boiled and broiled, stewed, baked and fried, and used an array of spices to make their dishes tasty. They had salt and a wide range of peppers, from hot red to gentle green. They also knew and used more exotic flavoring, such as vanilla and wild sage. What an Aztec family did not grow, raise, trap, snare or hunt itself, it could purchase at the market. Aztec markets were famous for their cleanliness, orderliness, and the variety of goods offered in them. This was true especially of the markets of Tenochtitlán, which make today's supermarkets look puny and sparse.

An anonymous conquistador, whose very anonymity made it possible for him to be an objective observer (he did not have to make points with the court at Castile, or proselytize for the church) describes the market as he saw it before Cortés razed the Aztec capital.

"The city of Tenochtitlán, Mexico, has large and very beautiful squares where every article in use among the people is offered for sale. The main square in particular, which is called Tutetula, is about three times the size of the square in Salamanca. There are porticoes around it, and every day about twenty to twenty-five thousand people are there buying and selling. On market day, which is held every five days, there are forty to fifty thousand people.

"There is an orderly arrangement of wares, so that each kind is sold separately in its proper place. The merchants who sell the goods are on one side of the square, and on the other side next to these are the ones who sell different kinds of stone mounted in gold, in the shape of birds and animals. In another part they sell mirrors and beads, and in another they have plumes and feathers of every color for sewing onto the dresses they wear for festivals and warfare. In another part they cut the stones for knives and swords, which is something very interesting to see, and they also

The famous central market of Tenochtitlán, the capital of the Aztec empire. The conquistadors were impressed by its variety and its organization.

make swords and shields. In another place they sell mantles and various kinds of men's dress, while women's dresses are sold elsewhere. There is a place for the sale of shoes, another for tanned deer hides and other animal hides, and devices made of hair that all the Indian women use for the head. Cotton is sold in yet another place, and grain here and bread there, of various kinds. They sell pies, turkeys, chickens and eggs and, nearby, hare, rabbits, deer, quail, ducks and geese. There is another place for wines of several kinds, and a place for various kinds of herbs. On one street they sell pepper, on another medicinal roots and herbs, of which they have a great number. There is a place for fruits of all kinds; another where they sell wood for houses, and nearby they have lime and stone. In short, everything is sold separately and systematically.

"In addition to this great square there are others, and markets throughout the city where foodstuffs are sold."

Walking or paddling to the market, the citizens of Tenochtitlán could enjoy the view of their splendid, well-planned, spotless city. (The Aztecs had drainage, aqueducts, and irrigation, and used water lavishly to scrub their houses and streets as well as themselves.) The same anonymous conquistador recounts that:

"The great city of Tenochtitlán has many beautiful and wide streets, although except for two or three main streets all the avenues are water on one side and earth on the other. The people walk on the dirt side or ride canoes on the water. The canoes are of concave wood, and large enough sometimes to carry five people comfortably. And so they go about, some on land and others on the water, conversing with each other."

In addition to conversing with each other, they could also feast their eyes on the houses of the rich that lined the main canals and causeways. We owe our knowledge of what that view must have been like to another conquistador, Francisco Clavigero, whose amazement prompted him to take quill in hand. Clavigero writes:

"The houses of the rich were of stone and lime with several tall chambers and great patios. The flat roofs were made of good wood, the walls were so well polished that the first Spaniards to see them thought they were made of silver. The floors were of mortar, perfectly levelled and polished. Many houses had towers and roof crests, an atrium with trees, and an orchard with pools. The largest houses had two doors, one leading to the street and the other to the canal or canoe passage. Neither entrance had wooden doors because doors were not used, since they believed their houses were well defended by the severity of their laws against thieves. To keep people from peering inside they had the entrance covered with a reed curtain."

Aztec society at its peak was very much a class society and dress had as much social significance as housing. Everyone was adequately and appropriately clothed, but attire became more lavish and colorful as the person wearing it ascended the social ladder. At their most basic, clothes consisted, for men, of a cotton mantle tied on the shoulder, with a breechclout beneath; for women, of a skirt tied with a sash and blouse that was really just two oblongs of cotton sewed together with holes cut out for the arms and the neck. In cool weather, cotton cloth was replaced by wool, gotten not from sheep, which the Aztecs did not know until the Spaniards introduced that animal to the Americas, but from the silky fur of the bellies of rabbit or hare. On their feet, the Aztecs wore sandals made of rope and hide, flat, but sometimes with a high guard at the heel.

The city folk living in the stone houses of Tenochtitlán elaborated on the same basic theme. The observant anonymous conquistador says:

"Their dress consists of cotton mantles like sheets, though not so large, finely worked in a variety of ways, and with decorated bands and borders. Each person has two or three, in red, black, white, purple and yellow. They cover their private parts, in front as well as in back, with very showy cloths like the large kerchiefs they put on their heads on journeys. They are of various colors, with trimmings of diverse colors also, and tassels that hang front and back. They wear shoes without vamps but only soles and highly decorated heels. Long laces run from the toes to the instep and are fastened there with buttons. They wear nothing on their heads except in combat or in their festivals and dances, and wear their hair long and tied in various ways."

And what about the clothes of Aztec women, to whom the anonymous but nevertheless gallant conquistador was obviously partial?

"The women," he reports appreciatively, "wear sleeveless cotton blouses long and full, with a great amount of fancy work and decorated borders and very handsome. They wear two or three, or even four of these, one of them longer than the others. . . . From the waist down, they wear another kind of dress of pure cotton which reaches to the knees, also very showy and finely worked. They wear nothing on the head, particularly in the cooler regions. They

have very beautiful hair, either black or brown, which they wear long. With their dresses, and their long flowing hair covering their backs, they are a beautiful sight."

Both men and women perfumed themselves, dyed and tattooed their faces and bodies, wore jewelry and carried flowers as an additional decorative touch for their costumes. Jewelry included necklaces and bracelets, ear, nose and lip plugs, mirrors and, for men on ceremonial occasions, headdresses. Jewelry was made of gold, silver, jade, semiprecious stones, beads, and shells. Some shell necklaces were worn not so much for their color or shape but for the gentle tinkling sound they made as the wearer walked along the causeway, or as the wind played on the necklace while the wearer traveled by canoe across the lake or along a canal in Tenochtitlán.

Dress reached its heights of elaborateness and splendor in the costume of the people on the top rung of the social ladder, the lords of Tenochtitlán.

Another surprised and impressed conquistador, Bernardino de Sahagún, provides a full-fashion commentary on these lordly habits.

"The prime ornamentation of the lords was called a *quetzalilpiloni,* two round tassels made of rich feathers with gold adornments, which they wore tied to the crown of the head. They wore on their arms gold bracelets, and golden earrings in their ears. Attached to the wrist was a thick black strap anointed with sweet-smelling balsam, and on it a thick bead of jade or other precious stone. They wore in the lower lip a jade bead set in gold, or some long pieces of rock crystal within which were stuck blue feathers, which made them seem like sapphires. They had their lower lip pierced and wore these ornaments hanging as though they came out of the flesh, and they also had some golden halfmoons hanging from these lip ornaments. The noses of the great lords were also pierced, to insert some fine turquoise or other precious stone.

"They wore chains of precious stones around their necks

Discipline, willpower, and self-control were hallmarks of the Aztec personality. All three are unmistakable in the face of this Aztec man.

or had a medallion hanging from a gold necklace, in the center of which was a beautiful polished stone, and around the circumference hung some pearl danglers. They wore mosaic bracelets, made of turquoise, some with rich plumes. They also wore on the lower part of the legs some thin gold bands. In the right hand they held a little golden flag, topped with feathers. They wore a bird headdress of feathers, with the beak coming over the head of the wearer, and the wings came down his temples. They also used flychasers made of feathers and gold, and on the left wrist some turquoise bracelets. Their necklaces were made of gold beads, separated by tiny marine shells. The lords held flowers in their hands, together with a smoke tube, on which they would suck. Each had a mirror in which he looked when he dressed himself, and which he gave to a page to be put away."

There are no comparably detailed accounts of how the ladies of the Aztec court were dressed, but pictorial evidence indicates that theirs was a somewhat less splendid attire. However, they, too, wore necklaces and bracelets, daubed themselves with long-lasting, sweet-smelling resin and carried bouquets of herbs or flowers carefully composed for both color and fragrance.

While the Aztecs were obnoxious to their neighbors, they had good manners within their own society. It was not the exquisite courtesy of the Maya based on a sensitivity to the needs and feelings of others; nor was it the thorough commitment of the Inca to play as well as they could the social role assigned to them by the benevolent and protective sovereign in Cuzco. Aztec manners emerged from the self-discipline and the fear of disapproval by peers and lords that a conquest-obsessed social system required and enforced.

There exists, in Aztec literature, a counterpart to the famous father-to-son advice in Shakespeare's Hamlet, which begins: "To thine own self be true, and it must follow as the night the day, thou cans't not then be false to any man."

The classic counsel of the Aztec father reverses this in-

The Aztecs cultivated a special breed of dog for food. It was hairless, like this one.

junction. It says, do what is expected of you, and you will live happily. The Aztec father's advice also indicates what was regarded as good manners in Aztec society. It reads:

"Revere and salute your elders and greet them properly. Console the poor with good deeds and kind words. Honor, love, serve and obey your parents. Do not follow madmen, who honor neither father nor mother. Do not mock the old, the sick, the crippled, or those in serious trouble, but humiliate yourself before the gods, and hope that the same will not happen to you. Do not dress too strangely, because this is a sign of little intelligence. Do not pull another by the hand or clothes, because this is a sign of frivolity. Do not enter or leave before your elders, nor cross in front of them, nor speak to them first. When you eat, give part of the food to him who comes begging it. If anything is given to you, no matter how little, do not despise it, or become angry, or think that you deserve more, because you lose character in the sight of the gods and man. Do not be a gambler or a thief, because the two go together and you will be dishonored in public places. Keep on the straight path, sow and reap, and eat of the produce of your own labor. Thus you will live happily, and your parents will love you."

There is also father-to-daughter parental counsel. It has an additional dimension of feeling, imagination, and philosophy, but the basic counsel is much the same as it is for the boy: do what is expected of you by god and man.

To his daughter, the fond father says: "Here you are, my little girl, my necklace of precious stones, my plumage, my human creation, born of me. You are my blood, my color, my image . . .

"Listen, look, understand, for thus it is on earth. Do not be idle, do not walk aimlessly, do not wander without destination. How should you live? How should you go on for a short time? They say it is very difficult to live on earth, a place of dreadful struggle, my little lady, my little bird, my little one . . .

"Look now at your work, that which you have to do: dur-

ing night and day, devote yourself to the things of God; think often how He is like the night and the wind. Pray to Him, invoke Him, call to Him, beg Him earnestly when you are in the place where you sleep. This way your sleep will be pleasant . . .

"Watch for the dawn, get up quickly, extend your hands, extend your arms, raise your face, wash your hands, cleanse your mouth, take up the broom quickly, begin to sweep. Do not be idle, do not stay there close to the fire, wash the mouth of your little brothers; burn *copal* incense, do not forget it, for thus you will have the mercy of Our Lord.

"And this being done, when you will be prepared, what will you do? How will you fulfill your womanly duties? Will you not prepare the food, the drink? Will you not spin and weave? Look well how are the food and drink, how they are made, that they should be good; know how good food and drink are prepared . . .

"Open well your eyes to see what is the art of feathers; how to embroider in colors and how to interweave the threads; how women dye them, those who are like you, our wives, the noble women. How they place the threads on the loom, how to make the woof of the cloth, how to hold it fast. Pay attention, apply yourself, be not idle, do not stand idly by, be strict with yourself . . .

"Prepare yourself; watch who is your enemy so that no one should make light of you. Do not give yourself to a wastrel, to one who seeks you for his own pleasure, a depraved boy. Nor should two or three faces you may have seen know you. Whoever may be your companion, you two must go to the end of life together. Do not leave him, hold to him, cling to him even though he be a poor man, even though he be only a small eagle, a small tiger, an unhappy soldier, a poor noble, sometimes tired, lacking goods; not for that do you neglect him . . .

"With these words from my mouth do I give all this to you. Thus before Our Lord, I fulfill my duty. And if perchance you cast this away, still you know it. I have fulfilled my duty, my little woman, my little daughter. May you be happy, may our Lord bring you success."

Aztec children were instructed, supervised, and trained to work from a very early age, just about as soon as they had learned to walk. The division of labor was rigid, with boys learning their fathers' traditional tasks and girls sharing the equally traditional labors of their mothers. If children strayed in any way from the carefully delineated path of morals and manners, punishment was swift and harsh. A small offense would bring a hard pinching of the arm or the ear, and if the transgression was repeated, it resulted in a parental assault on the same spot, this time with the sharp needle made from the spine of the maguey cactus. If the misdemeanor was grave, a child would be tied up and left outdoors overnight, shivering on the cold, hard ground. For a major offense—such as a girl speaking to a boy on the street—the punishment consisted of the parent starting a fire, throwing hot chili peppers into it, then pushing the child's face into the stinging smoke that inflamed the skin, chafed the nostrils and brought streams of tears from even the most disciplined and stoic Aztec youngster.

The tight discipline of the home was underlined and extended in school. The Aztecs had a system of universal education unique in human history until modern times. There is some question as to the age at which Aztec children started their educational process—some scholars say it was twelve, others hold it was fifteen—but there is no doubt that every Aztec boy and girl went to school.

The Aztecs had two kinds of educational institutions. One was the *Telpochcalli* (House of Youth) at which students were taught primarily martial arts if they were boys, domestic and healing arts if they were girls. But they were instructed as well in what we would today call civics, the history and customs, the religion and morals of their society, and in some of its arts including singing, dancing, and the playing of musical instruments.

Going to school in the Aztec empire was not a matter of hours. It took up the entire day and night, every day and night. School work and instruction started at dawn and continued till dusk. At sunset, students were allowed to go home to bathe, eat, and dress for the evening's activities, the "dressing" being essentially an application of the appropriate paint to their faces and bodies. Then they went back to school for an evening of instruction and performance in singing and dancing, in a special part of the school comparable to the assembly hall of today's high schools. The Aztecs called their assembly halls *Cuicalli,* the House of Song. Students stayed there until midnight, then returned to the telpochcalli to sleep. Telpochcalli dormatories consisted of the cold, hard ground, with each boy sleeping in his assigned portion of the clay floor, wrapped only in his light cotton mantle.

A boy would graduate in one of two ways: by getting married and taking up farming; or, a career considered infinitely more desirable, by going to war and capturing an enemy. If a student had been in battles a number of times without capturing a prisoner, he was considered a dunce, held in contempt and, eventually, kicked out of school. Leaving school on these terms meant that he could never hold a position of importance in the community and his inferior status was made visible to all by constraints on his attire. He was allowed to wear only the roughest cotton clothes and could never adorn himself with jewelry.

If the militaristic orientation of the Aztec educational system needed further emphasis, it was provided by the teachers, who earned their teaching certificates by capturing prisoners in battle. Telpochcallis were staffed by three kinds of teachers: instructors, chief instructors, and school directors, and a teacher's rank was determined by the number of prisoners he had provided for sacrifice to the sun.

The girls' teachers were priestesses and the chief discipline enforced in the girls' school, besides very hard work, was silence. The girls were not allowed to talk at meals, and "instruction" included long periods of mandatory silence. Girls' schools were enclosed by high walls. Girls were not allowed to leave the school, even to go home, without being accompanied by chaperones, who pinched them, or pricked them with maguey spines, if they raised their eyes.

Most of the girls graduated into marriage, but a few other choices were open to qualified women. They could become midwives, a profession that included other aspects of hygiene and healing. They could become marriage arrangers, a delicate and important task in Aztec society or, with additional training in a very special school, they could become priestesses.

Boys, too, had an institution of higher education. It was called *calmecac,* which means row of houses. The calmecac was clearly an elite institution, and its student body came mainly from the families of Aztec society's higher classes, although Aztec society did provide a degree of upward mobility for its talented youngsters from all classes. If a boy exhibited leadership qualities, defined by the Aztecs as courage, intelligence, and a capacity for self-discipline under normal as well as intensely stressful conditions, he was allowed to enter the calmecac even if he came from a family of poor farmers or petty dealers in chili peppers.

Calmecacs provided and trained the military, political, and religious leadership of the Aztecs.

Boys entered the calmecac at age fifteen, and stayed ten years. The training was rugged and many-faceted. As in the telpochcalli, the school day, combining work and instruction, began at dawn and lasted past midnight. But calmecac students could not go home for meals—they had to prepare their own food—and at midnight, when telpochcalli youngsters could finally get some well-earned sleep, calmecac students had to get up and pray and take a very cold bath.

The calmecac curriculum included all the subjects that were taught in the telpochcalli, but also offered instruction in the special knowledge required of an Aztec gentleman. This included rhetoric (calmecac students spoke *tecpil-*

latolli, a very precise, refined, and stylized form of the Nahuatl language); cartography, to meet the career requirements of both political and military leaders; science, which covered the study of the calendar and astronomy, botany, zoology, and the astrology and dream interpretation required by graduates who became priests; and art, which included painting, sculpture, architecture, and reading.

In Aztec society, reading was a multi-dimensional exercise. Aztec books consisted of pictographs accompanied by hieroglyphic text, and reading such a book required both an accurate interpretation of the pictogram and the correct understanding of the glyphs. Books dealt only with such important topics as Aztec history, genealogy, religious precepts and rituals, science, philosophy, and civic and moral instruction. They were read with the help of an instructor, who explained and commented, and accompanied the written text with an oral one, rhythmic and traditional, passed on unaltered from generation to generation. Calmecac students would repeat the oral text, in chorus, several times, to help them memorize it exactly. The exercise was known as "singing the pictures of the book."

CHAPTER FIVE

Flowers and Fortresses

RHETORIC and poetry were the arts most congenial to the Aztecs. They thought of poems as flowers and of the poet either as a person who composes flowers into garlands or as "an elegant bird who sings pictures."

As everything else in Aztec society, the writing and teaching of poetry was rigidly prescribed. There were special priests, called *tlapizcatzitzin,* who functioned as teachers, critics, and censors of poetry. If a person created a poem, word was sent to the tlapizcatzitzin who granted an audience to hear it. Singers were invited to the audience and, if the tlapizcatzitzin liked the composition, he would order the singers to perform it in rhythmic chorus. If that performance was successful, the poem became a part of the national patrimony. It was taught at the calmecac and, if the subject was suitable, at temple ceremonies. Words and rhythm were carefully, precisely preserved, with the tlapizcatzitzin in charge of, and responsible for, its pure preservation. Tlapizcatzitzin means "the conserver." Thus, while the poet was appreciated but forgotten, the poem achieved, within the Aztec time span, immortality.

In the realm of rhetoric, which the Aztecs prized as the acme of good breeding, standards were rigorous and perception was acute. The Aztecs knew exactly what they wanted—and did not want—from a speaker. They had a special word for a public speaker, *tlaquetzqui,* which means "one who makes things stand out." The tlaquetzqui, says an Aztec description, itself rhythmically coached, is:

Witty; he says things with spirit
With the lips and mouth of an artist.
The good speaker
Utters pleasing words, joyful words
Has flowers on his lips.
His speech overflows with counsel
Flowers come from his mouth.
His speech is pleasing and joyful as flowers.
From him come noble language
And careful sentences.

And here is the Aztec conception of a bad speaker:

The bad speaker
Uses slovenly language
And confuses words
Swallows them, speaks indistinctly
Narrates awkwardly, describes clumsily
Says useless words.
The bad speaker
Is without dignity.

While the Aztecs were not themselves profuse creators of original art in any field—their society was too rigid and too single-minded to allow for the freedom and diversity that makes originality possible—they became subtle and sophisticated appreciators of the arts of others. In characteristic Aztec style, they indulged their appreciation by writing imaginary artistic ancestors into their past and by commandeering live ones from the territories they had conquered.

One of the Aztec chronicles that survived the Spanish passion for book burning in the sixteenth century, the *Codice Matritense de la Real Academia,* describes these imaginary ancestors (they were probably Olmecs whom the Aztecs decided to appropriate for reasons of cultural prestige) as:

Those who carried with them
The black and red ink
The manuscripts and painted books
The wisdom.
They brought everything with them:
The annals,
The books of song,
And their flutes.

The Toltecs, from whom the Aztecs claimed blood lineage, appeared later in the Aztecs' manufactured history. The Toltec claim was extremely important because contained in it was the legend of Quetzalcoatl, the Feathered Serpent, who was both a historic personage and a cultural and religious symbol to all the pre-Columbian civilizations of Middle America.

It has been speculated that the historic Quetzalcoatl may have been a Viking. He may have come from the sea in the East, lived for some time among the people he encountered, and taught them Viking skills which, because they were unknown, seemed miraculous, and then left to go home, or as all the Quetzalcoatl legends say, walked into the sea.

The Aztec reach for Toltec identification was therefore not unlike the aspirations of the Teutonic Knights. But it contained artistic elements as well. As another surviving Aztec chronicle says:

The Toltecs, the people of Quetzalcoatl
Were very skillful.
Nothing was difficult for them to do.
They cut precious stones
Wrought gold
And made works of art
And marvelous ornaments of feathers.
Truly they were skillful.

In addition to appreciating art, the Aztecs also knew the kind of character and character training it took to produce an artist. Here is an Aztec profile of the creative person and the creative process:

The artist: disciplined, abundant, multiple, restless.
The true artist: capable, practicing, skillful.
Maintains a dialogue with his heart
Meets matters with his mind.
The true artist draws out all from his heart
Works with delight
Makes things calm, with sagacity . . .
Arranges materials; adorns them; makes them adjust.

With this range of appreciation, Tenochtitlán, in its imperial days, was probably a rewarding place for an artist. We do not know whether the artists from neighboring realms—Maya, Mixtec, Olmec descendants from the coast, Cholula craftsmen from the north—came to Tenochtitlán by choice, were dragooned there, or lured there by power, but we do know that a large number of artists and craftsmen lived and worked in Tenochtitlán from the last decades of the fifteenth century to the time the Spaniards toppled the Aztec empire and crushed its priests and poets, princes and painters. The artists who flocked to Tenochtitlán during that final period before the fall, included Mixtecs, who brought the skills of feather mosaics, metal casting and goldwork, wood carving and the working of precious stones.

Featherworkers in the Aztec empire were organized in a guild. Their output was in great demand for shields and cloaks, curtains, and headdresses.

The most famous crown in pre-Columbian history was a splendid artifact of feather mosaic. This was Montezuma's crown, a brilliant headdress of glowing green quetzal feathers that spread five feet in each direction, set on a mosaic base of blue, brown, and gold, with a separate mosaic of matching colors in the center. This core composition fulfilled the same attention-riveting function that the center jewel did in the crown of the kings of Spain. Except that Montezuma's crown had the extra attraction of swaying gently, with a soft, mysterious rustle, in even the faintest breeze. Montezuma gave this treasure to Cortés, as a gift for his sovereign, Charles V, who was also head of the Holy Roman Empire, which included Austria. The crown of Montezuma found its way to a Vienna museum, where it can still be seen today.

The National Museum of Mexico has a magnificent copy. It is an impressive sight but one wonders how any person could have balanced it on his head while moving or even just sitting on a throne.

Along with this headdress, Montezuma sent to Spain another sample of Aztec featherwork: a round, mosaic shield, with a blue coyote in the center, outlined with gold on a rose-colored background.

The featherwork was done in one of two ways: either by gluing large feathers on a piece of soft cloth and then superimposing carefully selected small ones to make a pattern; or by weaving and sewing bits of feathers directly into a backing.

The mosaic technique was also used in compositions of precious and semiprecious stone. Jewelry was one use for such mosaics, but they were also used for weapons, usually for ceremonial purposes, and, if a knight was prominent enough, for status identification as well. They were the Aztec equivalent of the jeweled sword handles sported by the knights of Europe, or the precious stone-encrusted sabers of the sultans and satraps of the Moslem world. One surviving example of a jewel-mosaic of this kind is a ceremonial knife with a flesh-colored blade of shiny quartz and a wooden handle, inset with malachite, turquoise, white, orange, pink and red shell, pyrites and jet, composed to depict an eagle knight in full regalia, looking appropriately ferocious, ready to pounce and slash. The mosaic constitutes an impressive portrait.

Goldwork among the Aztecs was used entirely for personal and symbolic ornamentation. Gold was hammered, shaped, filigreed into pendants and nose rings, earplugs, necklaces, rings, leg ornaments, artifacts that dangled from the sandal or glowed in the hair, pendants, breastplates and belt buckles, masques and figurines, as well as fan handles and vessels. It was used in the war implements of knights, ornamenting shields, spear throwers, knives, even armor. And it was used for ceremonial purposes. Among the many gifts Montezuma gave to Cortés for his faraway sovereign in Castile was a set of worked golden discs, the size of a cartwheel, representing the sun and the moon. Like most gifts of gold to reach Castile, these were melted down in the cauldrons of the Spanish mint to swell the gold hoard of the empire, in the process casually and cruelly obliterating the art of the American civilizations encountered by the conquistadors.

The products of Aztzc woodcarving, another well-developed craft, perished under the impact of natural forces but enough samples have survived to give us an idea of approach and style. The most exquisite examples of the craft seem to have been the carving of lintels and door posts, but the Aztec had limited appreciation for that application. They reserved their most elaborate carvings for implements of war and worship, for knives and spears and for the two-sided drums that set the rhythm for ceremonial sacrifices and the big stand-up drums sounded in the call for war.

Aztec sculpture was very realistic, sometimes crude. This owl is an example of Aztec realism.

Among the domestic arts, weaving and pottery were the most important. In this area, too, the Aztecs drew on the skills and techniques of all their subject peoples. With these sources at their disposal, the Aztecs knew how to do batik, tie-dyeing, and embroidery, how to make velvet, brocade, and many kinds of textile decoration. Their own preference was for geometric shapes or naturalist reproductions of plants and flowers. They also made clothes that imitated, in color, pattern and texture, the skins of animals.

Aztec pottery was surprisingly delicate, but it, too, was essentially derivative. It came to Tenochtitlán from Cholula, where the Puebla civilization had created a thin orange ware, decorated with light, curvaceous designs in a pale gray or a deep gray-black. Aztec adaptation coarsened the color to a heavy, glossy red, and changed the decoration from cursive and feathery scrolls, dots, and stylized serpent heads first to squared abstractions and later to naturalistic design showing birds and fish, butterflies and insects. Among the birds the eagle was paramount, and the transition after the conquest from the Aztec eagle with the serpent in its beak perched on the cactus to the double-headed eagle of the Spanish court was an easy one. The conquistadors were impressed by the bold, realistic, imperial eagle Aztec potters produced on bowls, vases, and plates after the Spaniards came.

The Aztecs never managed to do much with painting, perhaps because, as a true art, it cannot be dragooned or copied. They had the splendid examples of mural painting in the Maya world to the south and the colorful and delightful heritage of Teotihuacán, but Aztec efforts to reproduce either were clumsy. One knowledgeable critic of Mesoamerican art says Aztec painting was "crabbed and conventional," but it was even worse than that. It was at the level of a comic strip, both in its architectural use and in the illustrated codices.

A model of the central plaza of Tenochtitlán, the Aztec capital, at the time of the conquest. It is now the main square of Mexico City.

The arts in which the Aztecs did best were architecture, with its subsidiary techniques of engineering; urban planning; agricultural skills; and stone sculpture.

The most monumental expressions of Aztec architectural ideas and skills were their temples, tall, truncated pyramids usually with twin sanctuaries at the top. The Great Pyramid at Tenochtitlán had broad flights of stairs sweeping upward toward a flattened top, crowned by a sanctuary for Huitzilopochtli, painted flame-red with a frieze of white cranes, and a twin temple for Tlaloc, the rain god, painted water-blue and white. The contrast must have been dramatic, with further impact lent to the spectacle by the Aztec notion that the more powerful a god, the bigger a temple he deserved. The sanctuary at Tenochtitlán was high and, in the pellucid air of Mexico's Central Valley, may well have appeared to reach into the sky. This was especially true for spectators congregated in the temple courtyard below.

G. C. Vaillant, a U.S. expert on the Aztecs, describes the effect of the main pyramid of Tenochtitlán as he imagines it to have been:

"The planes between the temple's terraces are so cunningly calculated that the observer standing at the foot of the great staircase cannot see people at the top. He is conscious only of the massive ascent disappearing into space. When the stairs were used by a religious procession, in all its pomp and color, the effect must have been stupendous. The elaborate hierarchy of a great civilization moved upwards to meet, at a point unseen by the beholders, the infinity of the heavens, concentrated aloft in the god's image."

The twin temples that the spectators on the ground could see were square, sturdy, massive, and had the air of fortresses, as if even the gods had to barricade themselves against the onslaught of the elements and be ready to do battle at all times. Indeed, that is what the Aztecs believed.

At a more mundane level, the Aztecs were skilled engineers and versatile planners. They constructed dikes and aqueducts, canals and bridges, drainages and sewer systems. They built elevated causeways, usually leading arrow-straight into the four cardinal directions. They diverted water for irrigation, and they invented two unique ways to create arable plots, which were as decorative as they were original. These produced the famous *chinampas,* the floating gardens that survive to this day. Chinampas are artificial islands constructed in swamps or shallow waters, which are particularly fertile because the plant roots reach into the moisture below and are nourished by both water

The famous "Aztec calendar." It is really a stone sculpture of Aztec religious myths and symbols.

and minerals. There is speculation that the Aztecs brought the technique with them from their origins in the swamps of the north, where they watched cranes dip their heads into the water and invariably come up with an edible creature or blade. Another version of the *chinampa* is a raft made of poles, with layers of rich lake soil piled on top, in which the Aztecs planted flowers, creating floating islands of fragrance and brilliance in the center and along the rim of the lake.

Even the Spaniards were impressed.

"When we saw so many cities built in the water," conquistador Bernal Díaz writes, "and other great towns on dry land, and that straight causeway going toward Tenochtitlán, we were amazed and said that it was like the enchantments they tell of in the legend of Amadis. And some of our soldiers even asked whether the things we saw were not a dream!"

The achievements of the Aztecs may well have seemed like a dream to the Spaniards, but for the people who lived in Tenochtitlán or under the rule of Tenochtitlán, existence was at least as much a nightmare as it was a dream. The Aztecs' other major artistic achievement, sculpture, reflects this. Aztec monumental sculpture is either historic or religious and in either case depicts terror along with fertility, blood and death preceding—and following—rain and dawn.

The most famous of the Aztec historic sculptures to survive is "the Stone of Tizoc," a monument of basalt, shaped like a drum, its rim elaborately carved to depict major events in the reign of Tizoc, fifth ruler of the Aztecs. It is the Aztec equivalent to the monuments of a conqueror on his steed with which the Spaniards studded the Americas in their day. The Spanish monuments usually show a proud soldier on a prancing horse; the stone of Tizoc shows, more realistically, soldiers confronting and killing each other; prisoners being dragged by the hair; shields being thrust aside in mortal combat; great feather headdresses being wrenched off and fluttering to the ground.

Of the great religious sculptures, the most horrendously impressive is the mammoth statue of the earth goddess Coatlicue sporting fangs and adorned with a necklace and bracelet of human hearts and skulls. The most inspired and inspiring is the stone disk known—inadequately—as "The Aztec Calendar," which is really the essence of Aztec religion carved into rock, quite comparable in its own frame of reference to the tablets incised with the ten commandments that Moses brought down from the mountain in the desert of Sinai.

CHAPTER SIX

Smoking Mirror, Feathered Serpent

THE tale told by the Aztec calendar—the present-day descendants of the Aztecs call it the Stone of the Sun—concerns the cosmic origin of man. The Aztecs believed that the world had been created and destroyed four times before the present age, which they called the age of the sun, or the age of movement, movement referring to the stars and planets whose rhythmic travels they observed in the sky.

The first of the four previous ages was the age of the jaguar during which the earth was populated by giants. The deity that presided over that age was Tezcatlipoca, the Smoking Mirror, who in Aztec mythology holds a place comparable to that of Satan in the Judeo-Christian faith. But the Aztecs' Tezcatlipoca resembles Satan not so much in his role as the symbol of evil, but in his aspect of the fal-

A jaguar, sculpted by an Aztec. Its realistic likeness is very different from the symbolic richness of an Olmec depiction of the same creature.

len angel, a brightness tarnished, a smoking mirror. When the first age ended with the jaguars devouring the giants, Tezcatlipoca transformed himself into a sun.

The second age was the age of the wind and the god that ruled over that age was Quetzalcoatl, the Feathered Serpent. Quetzalcoatl was the mirror image of the Smoking Mirror, a creature born lowly, slithering on its belly on the ground, but with wings so it could fly and reach the heavens. The Feathered Serpent represented to the Aztecs the highest aspiration of man. The age of the wind blew to its end in a gigantic hurricane from which only a handful of men escaped alive. These creatures sought refuge in trees and were converted into monkeys.

The third age was the age of rain, with Tlaloc, the rain god, giving the earth light and moisture. It ended with a "fiery rain," probably the mythical description of an erupting volcano. The only way humans could escape that catastrophe was by climbing up high on some of the nonvolcanic mountains that ring the Valley of Mexico. Those who did so were turned into birds.

The fourth age was the age of water, the reign of the goddess Chalchiutlicue, Our Lady of the Turquoise Skirt. Her era was destroyed by a flood, and the only way some human creatures could survive it was by being turned into a fish.

The fifth age, which the Aztecs considered their own, therefore began with monkeys, fish, and birds but no more giants. It was preceded by a period of darkness and silence, when there was no sun nor any human life. It began when Tonatiuh, the sun god, whose image occupied the center of the Aztec calendar, took over the universe. It would end, the Aztecs believed, shattered by earthquakes, and human beings would die of starvation. As one Aztec manuscript—the Annals of Cuauhititlan—says:

This Sun, its name is Four-Movement
This is our Sun
In which we now live . . .

It is called the Sun of Movement
Because it moves, follows its course.
And the old ones, the wise ones, go about
saying
There will be earthquakes
There will be hunger
And thus we will perish.

The conviction that their existence would inevitably come to a violent end infused Aztec life with melancholy and terror. Much of their life was devoted to appeasing the gods, in the hope of staving off misery and tragedy by rounds of ritual and chains of sacrifice. The Aztecs perceived divinities all around them. Whatever they did not understand or could not control became a major or minor god. As one disgusted conquistador observed: "There was nothing living of any kind or species that was not worshipped as a god, even butterflies, lobsters and fleas."

This was not true for all Aztecs, however. The educated, spiritually sophisticated elite, consisting primarily of priests and nobles, had evolved religious concepts that do not differ very much from our own. They believed in a monotheistic creator whose divine presence was everywhere, at all times. They called him Tloque Nahuaque, the God of the Near Vicinity.

This elite had also conceived of a kind of divine Adam and Eve, a celestial pair they called Ometecuhtli and Omecihuatl, who were the parents of the other major divinities in the Aztecs' richly populated pantheon.

For the Aztec people, the denizens of the pantheon who really mattered were those that affected their daily lives. The most important were the rain god Tlaloc, he who makes things grow, and his wife, the Lady of the Turquoise Skirt. Their effect on mankind is described in a legend retold by Alfonso Caso, a contemporary Mexican expert on Aztec mythology. The legend says that Tlaloc and the Lady of the Turquoise Skirt live in a house with four rooms and a large patio in the middle. Four large jars of water stand in the patio. The water in one jar is very good and from it come the rains that make seeds sprout. In another jar, the water is bad and when the rains come from that jar, cobwebs form on the grain and the grain mildews. The third jar contains water that sends freezing rains and the fourth jar sends the rains that cause the grain to decay.

According to the legend, the divine couple did not itself dip into the four jars and send one of the four rains down to mankind. Instead, Tlaloc and his lady created a multitude of priests with tiny bodies who live in their house and hold small pots in one hand, in which they draw water from the four jars. In the other hand they hold sticks. When Tlaloc or the Lady of the Turquoise Skirt command them to go and take rain to certain areas, they fetch their pots and their sticks and pour down the water the rain gods have ordered. "And when it thunders, that is when they break their pots with the sticks, and when the lightning flashes, that is because of what they had in the pots."

As important as Tlaloc and his spouse, but in a very different way, was Huitzilopochtli, the god of fire, who by extension was also the sun and the god of life. Huitzilopochtli was the Aztecs' tribal deity who had brought them from their primitive life in the marshlands, through decades of wandering, to Tenochtitlán; had commanded them to become conquerors of the valley; and had inspired them to build their empire and to expand it infinitely. The Aztecs considered themselves "The People of the Sun" with a mission to assure that Huitzilopochtli was supplied always with the only nourishment worthy of him, "the precious liquid," human blood. It was to secure this nourishment that the Aztecs kept fighting and conquering. Their goal was the procurement of prisoners by the thousands, at the height of their power by the tens of thousands, who became sacrificial victims in Aztec temples, their "precious liquid" offered to Huitzilopochtli to keep him content and thus make certain that the sun continued to shine on all mankind.

A happier god was Xochipilli, "the Prince of Flowers," who was kept company by his lovely wife Cochiquetzal, "the Feathered Flower." Xochipilli was a combination of the Greeks' Apollo and Dionysus, a god of love and song, games and dance. His wife was the goddess of beauty and love. Both were the guardian gods of the Aztecs who cultivated chinampas.

Another deity of the good things in life was Xipe, god of spring, of everything green and growing and, by extension, god of renewal. In the Aztec tradition of paying the highest possible price for favors received from the gods, Xipe was also known as "the flayed one," because the priests who served him paid their ritual tribute to this god of renewal by dressing themselves in the skins of sacrificial victims who had been flayed. In its essence, the gesture was of a kind with the masques used by the Greeks or the costumes worn in a morality play in Europe during the Middle Ages. Only in their ritual, the Aztecs always went that last mile to the deadly end: they used human skin, and only human sacrifice would do in appeasing, placating, imploring, and nourishing the gods.

The same attitude turned the major female goddess, Coatlicue, from an earth mother into an earth monster. In most religions, the principal female deity is either a goddess of fertility, ample and succulent, or a symbol of purity, graceful and contained. Coatlicue was neither. Massive and square, she was adorned with human skulls and bones, wearing a long necklace of human hands and hearts and a girdle fastened with a skull. Her skirt was made of writhing snakes and her feet and arms ended in claws. Coatlicue means "the Lady of the Skirt of Serpents."

As the basic mother goddess, Coatlicue had another as-

pect, with another name. Her other name was Cihuacoatl and, under that appellation, she was the goddess both of women who died in childbirth (in Aztec belief, such women went straight to a special paradise of their own) and of newborn children. Her priests read the horoscopes of newborn babies and decided when a child should be named to make certain that its life conformed to what the stars had decreed.

Another important goddess was Tlazolteotl, "the Goddess of Filthy Things." She often carries a broom in her hands. But her important function was as goddess of confession. The filthy things she took upon herself were the sins of men. An Aztec could make a confession to the priests of Tlazolteotl and receive absolution. The power of the goddess was such that once a person had made confession and done the penance decreed by Tlazolteotl's priests, no punishment could be meted out by the state for that confessed crime. The assumption was that if the goddess had forgiven, so must society. There was a proviso, however, that makes this seemingly generous approach not at all as permissive as it appears. An Aztec could confess to Tlazolteotl only once in a lifetime.

Also important to the death-haunted Aztecs were Mictlantecuhtli and Mictecacihuatl, the lord and lady of the underworld, whose faces were covered with masks made of skulls and whose ornaments were human bones. They lived in the heart of the underworld, a place called Chignahumictlan. Every Aztec, except those who had died as warriors or sacrificial victims, in childbirth or by drowning, ended up in the domain of Mictlantecuhtli and Mictecacihuatl.

The Aztecs' notion of the structure of the universe was complex. They believed that there were thirteen heavens and nine layers of underworld, with all kinds of cosmic

The Aztec goddess of fertility has a ferocious aspect.
She was believed to destroy as well as nourish.

events taking place in each. The eleventh heaven, for example, was red and belonged to the god of fire; the tenth was yellow and the domain of the sun gods; the ninth was white and constituted the realm of the evening star. Closer to home, the second heaven was where all the other stars lived, along with the gods of the night sky and the Milky Way. The first heaven, which was closest to earth, was where the clouds took shape, the moon set off for his daily stroll, and the planets roamed.

Man's fate after death was not a simple matter either. In Aztec belief, the soul after death set out on a journey in one of four directions. If a man died in war, or as a sacrificial victim—and this applied whether he was Aztec or enemy—he went east to a paradise called Tonatiuhichan, which means "the house of the sun." There, he would live on as the constant companion of the sun, whose arrival each morning he would greet with shouts of joy and the beating of his shield. He would live in a garden filled with flowers and spend his days fighting sham battles. If he wanted to pay a visit to earth he could do so in the form of a hummingbird or another flying creature with brilliant plumage. On these earthly visits he could feed on the nectar of earth flowers before returning to the house of the sun. As an Aztec told one of the friars who came to Mexico very shortly after the conquest:

"The ancient ones said that the Sun calls them [the warriors and sacrificial victims] unto him, so that they can gladden his heart and sing in his presence and give him pleasure. They share a life of continued delight with him. They enjoy constant pleasures and taste and sip the nectar of all sweet-tasting and sweet-smelling flowers. Never do they feel sad or experience any pain or sorrow, because they live in the mansion of the Sun, where there is an abundance of delights."

Women who died in childbirth went west, to a paradise

called Cincalo, the house of corn, where they lived on forever with ample food at their disposal.

Those who died by drowning—Tlaloc, the rain god, was often propitiated by the ritual drowning of men, or, more often, women and children in lakes or deep wells—went south, to Tlaloc's paradise, Tlalocan. Tlalocan was a delightful place, with fruit-laden trees, growing along the banks of rivers and lagoons where the residents played water games and sang to each other. An enchanting mural depicting the joys of Tlalocan has been found and restored in a palace some thirty miles from Mexico City, near the temples of Teotihuacán.

For those Aztecs who did not qualify for one of the three paradises, the road after death led north to Mictlan, the underworld. It was a demanding journey. First the dead had to cross a deep river, the Chignahuapan. The Greeks had a similar belief about the crossing of the river Styx, but in Greek mythology a boatman rowed the dead person across. In Maya mythology, where the dead also had to cross a river, they could row themselves. In Aztec belief he had to cross the river on his own. Aztecs were often buried with a dog in their tomb, the assumption being that the dog would help his master cross the river.

Having crossed the river, the soul arrived in the second underworld, where it had to make its way over two mountains that were joined together. In the third underworld, it had to climb a mountain made of obsidian, a sharp, hard volcanic glass. In the fourth underworld the soul was assailed by an icy wind, so cold and cutting that it felt like obsidian blades. In the fifth underworld, the soul had to find its way through a maze of flapping flags. In the sixth, it was pierced by arrows. The seventh underworld was inhabited by wild beasts that feasted on human hearts. In the eighth, the dead had to negotiate a narrow path set between high boulders. By the time they arrived in the final, ninth underworld, Chignahumictlan, where Mictlantecuhutli and Mictecacihuatl, the lord and lady of the underworld, held

Another Aztec version of Tlaloc, the rain god. The eyes, the mouth, the earplugs are all shaped like raindrops.

court, they were exhausted. In Chignahumictlan, the souls found their final rest or disappeared forever.

In a society so deeply haunted in life and death by exacting, capricious divinities, religious ritual played an important role. And those in charge of ritual, priests and priestesses, were deeply feared and greatly respected.

An Aztec poem describes the priestly role and how the people felt about their clergy.

There are those who guide us
They govern us, they carry us upon their backs
And instruct us how the gods must be worshipped . . .
The experts, the knowers of speeches and orations.
It is their duty
To busy themselves day and night
With the placing of incense
With their offering
With the thorns to draw their blood.
Those who see
Those who dedicate themselves to observing
The movements and the orderly operations of the heavens
How the night is divided.

The clergy was organized in a hierarchy headed by the emperor himself, who assumed some priestly functions. The full-time priests with the most important rank and role were the Quetzalcoatl-Totec and the Quetzalcoatl-Tlaloc, representing respectively Huitzilopochtli, the deity of fire—and by tradition the Aztecs' leader and mentor—and Tlaloc, the rain god. Both had sanctuaries on the crest of the main pyramid of Tenochtitlán, and the high priests who served them were at the top of the ecclesiastical pyramid.

Ranking immediately below these two high priests was the empire's chief clerical administrator, the Mexicatl Teohuatzin. He was in charge of religious affairs in the Aztecs' own realm as well as in all the conquered provinces. He was also the top bureaucrat of the Aztec clergy. His two deputies, Huitznahuac Teohuatzin and Tepanteo-huatzin, were in charge of the educational system throughout the realm, both the tellochcalli, the elementary schools most Aztec youngsters attended, and the calmecac, the special institute for the gifted. The deputies in turn had two major assistants, the Ometotochtzin and the Tlapitzcaltzin. The former served the god of pulque, the Aztecs' chief intoxicant, and the latter served the god of music. Tlapitzcaltzin means "the Lord of the House of Flutes." Together, these two priests presided over a unique institution, the *cuicacalli,* a kind of academy of music, where sacred songs, and the instruments that accompanied sacred song in priestly ritual, were taught.

Beneath this clerical elite was the sizable corps of working priests, divided again into three layers. The top layer were the *Tlanamacac,* roughly equivalent to the level of the monsignor in the Catholic Church. Next below this were the equivalent to the parish priests, the *Tlamacazqui.* At the bottom of the hierarchy were the *Tlamacazton,* the young men just graduated from the calmecac, who served in temples as novices.

For these three bottom rungs in the clerical hierarchy, there was a parallel structure for women, with priestesses serving the major female deities and fulfilling also the tasks of teachers and supervisors in the special schools for girls.

In their various ranks and capacities, Aztec priests were, therefore, in charge of all facets of Aztec education and ritual. They also kept the Aztec calendar, a complex process of reckoning time by the physical revolution of the earth on its axis in conjunction with a shorter, mathematically designed calendar of sacred days. The priestly time count served to determine the seasons and therefore the times for sowing and harvesting, while the sacred calendar governed the individual's fate. Between them, the two reckonings included all that was vital in the life of an Aztec whose attachment to the priests was therefore profound and inescapable. Priests also devised and interpreted the Aztecs' picture books which taught the myth and legends of the race and guarded and transmitted the special, elegant language that was taught in the calmecac.

Finally, priests accompanied Aztec troops to war and led them in battle.

In religious ceremonies, the priestly role was one of leadership rather than of exclusive performance. The Aztec congregation actively participated in religious worship by singing, dancing, jingling bells, blowing on rasping whistles, and making music with clay flutes and bone rattles, shells, trumpets and animal-skin-covered double drums. At the great temple of Tenochtitlán, crowned by the sanctuaries of Tlaloc and Huitzilopochtli, as many as 5,000 persons would attend a religious ceremony and join the priests in beseeching and cajoling the gods.

For the Aztecs any dialogue with the divinities required blood. It could be as little as a drop obtained by pricking their own bodies with a cactus thorn or an obsidian blade. It could be the symbolic sacrifice of such a person as a ballplayer who had lost a game, or a noble prisoner who went to his death playing a flute as he mounted the steps to the sacrificial stone. Or it could be a horrendous bloodbath, the ritual massacre of literally thousands of men, women, and children, when the need was felt to either appease the gods in some particularly urgent and compelling way or to offer them thanks in an extravagant fashion. History is not dependable on this, but there are claims that the Aztecs killed as many as 25,000 persons on a single occasion.

History is dependable, however, in relating the meaning that human sacrifice had for the Aztecs and the reverence that accompanied the killing. A conquistador who personally witnessed a sacrificial ceremony describes it:

An Aztec chac mol, *the special altar designed for human sacrifice.*

"First the person who is to be sacrificed is finely adorned and led with much gaiety and festivity through the streets and squares where the people tell him their wants, saying that since he is going where their god is, he can ask him to help them. They give him food or some other gift and in this way he gathers many things, but everything goes to the sacrificers.

"They take him to the temple, where they hold a great festival with dances, in which he also joins. Later, one of the priests who is to kill him undresses him and leads him to one side of the temple stairs where there is a stone idol. He lays him on his back, tying his hands on either side and then his feet. Again they all start singing and dancing around him telling him the message he is to carry to their god.

"Next comes the sacrificer, whose office is not the least among them, and he takes a stone blade that cuts like steel and is the size of a large knife. In the time it would take one to make the sign of the cross, he thrusts the knife into the victim's chest and opens it, and takes out the heart while it is still hot and beating. It is immediately taken by the supreme pontiff, who anoints the mouth of the principal idol with the blood, and, without pausing, casts some of the blood toward the sun or a star if it is night. Then the mouths of the other stone and wooden idols are anointed, and the cornice of the chapel door where the principal idol is. After this they burn the heart, keeping the ashes as a relic, and also burn the victim's body, the ashes of which are kept in a different vessel from those of the heart.

"At other times they sacrifice them without these preliminaries and burn the heart and the bones of the arms and legs and keep them wrapped in many folds of paper as great relics . . .

"They are the most devout people in the observance of their religion that God ever created, to such an extent that they offer themselves voluntarily to be sacrificed, thinking to save their souls in this way."

CHAPTER SEVEN

Rich Man, Poor Man, Merchant, Judge

IN their political and economic life, the Aztecs started out as a simple, democratic society, in which each clan elected its own officials and power flowed up from the people to the ruler, who provided both religious and secular leadership. Later, as the empire grew, Aztec society became more complex and rigid. Increasingly, it solidified into classes, with specific privileges, and not much leeway for an individual to move from one class to another. As this happened, the political system changed from a democracy to an autocracy, with officials at every level appointed rather than elected, and with the power flow reversed, emanating from what had become a hereditary imperial family supported by phalanxes of warriors and priests.

In the early democratic days, the basic social unit was the *calpulli,* composed of 50 to 100 families. The calpulli was subdivided into a number of neighborhoods, called *tlaxilacalli,* which means blocks of houses. Tlaxilacalli consisted of large families that cultivated their land in common.

The calpulli held in trust communal lands, which it assigned to families according to need. Each calpulli had its own name, its own school, its own government. It also had its own patron deity and its own flag and insignia when it joined the Aztec armed forces in battle.

The political system of an Aztec calpulli was not unlike that of an early New England community, with a town council headed by selectmen and a form of town hall meeting at which issues facing the community were discussed and problems thrashed out and solved.

The Aztec calpulli was governed by a council composed of heads of families, or family groups, usually an old and presumably wise representative of each family group. It met every twenty days to discuss calpulli affairs and devise solutions to calpulli problems. If an emergency arose a special session could be called.

The council elected the calpulli's officials, who were entrusted with specific functions. The two main elected officials were the *Techuhtli* (captain), who was a military man and was responsible for the calpulli's military needs and obligations. His duties ranged from training youngsters to leading the calpulli's contingent in battle. The other elected official—he served for life—was the *Teachcautin* (the title means "oldest relative"), who was responsible for the calpulli's civic needs. He was in charge of administration, law and order, the distribution of lands and their produce, and such civil works as roads and bridges. To help him with his assortment of tasks, he appointed other calpulli members to function as work supervisors, teachers, policemen, or administrative aides. These appointments were honorary and temporary, and went to people respected in the calpulli for their competence and rectitude. The assignments were usually discharged in addition to the person's job, constituting a kind of moonlighting in the service of the community. They were not voluntary. No Aztec would have dreamt of refusing an assignment from the teachcautin.

The teachcautin presided over the calpulli council and represented the calpulli in the next echelon of government, the *tlatocan,* or place of discourses. The tlatocan was the equivalent of a town meeting, and a township was simply a collection of calpulli. The township, in addition to the house of discourse, had an array of officials who were elected by the tlatocan. There were four main executive officers who, between them, settled whatever disputes arose between the various calpulli, and who pulled together the military power of the calpulli when it was needed. Reflective of the Aztecs' tough and militaristic society even at that stage, two of the four officials were entrusted with judicial affairs, the third was an executioner and the fourth served as a liaison officer between the community's civil and military establishments. The four were assisted by a number of specialized functionaries who, at the tlatocan level, held their jobs on a full-time basis. They included tax collectors, scribes, supervisors of communal labor, policemen, advocates, judges, market administrators and priests.

The tlatocan's four top executives also served as royal electors and, in the early democratic days, as the king's counselors.

But Aztec democracy shrank as the empire expanded. By the time the conquistadors encountered the Aztecs, their society was locked into a tight hierarchy of eleven distinct classes. Starting from the top, they were: the reigning monarch and his family; the nobility; professional warriors; priests; merchants; craftsmen; the bureaucracy; independent farmers who were Aztecs by birth; farmers in the conquered territories; bearers, whose entire life consisted of carrying burdens on their backs from one corner of the empire to another, often requiring a trip of 200 to 300 miles with loads of as much as 100 pounds; and, finally, slaves.

Illustrating the finely drawn hierarchical divisions into

which Aztec society had deteriorated by the time the Spaniards arrived, was the fact that slaves were divided into four subclasses of their own. There were military slaves, who had been captured in battle and, for some reason, had escaped the customary fate of being sacrificed in a triumphal temple ceremony. Such slaves were either kept as domestic servants by rich or ruling families, or were put to work on some communal enterprise, especially if it required particularly arduous labor. Then there were criminal slaves, people who had been convicted of an offense that did not call for the death penalty. The Aztecs did not believe in keeping such criminals in jails; instead, they required them to make restitution to the individual or family that had been harmed by their crime. They were assigned as slaves to the injured party and put to work in whatever way the people against whom the crime had been committed saw fit. They were privately owned by the individual they had harmed.

Finally, there were two kinds of voluntary slavery, one economically induced and the other psychologically prompted. Poor or landless persons who saw no way of feeding themselves would offer themselves as slaves, and sometimes a family with many children would sell a child into slavery. Occasionally, too, a destitute family requiring a loan from a more fortunate member of the calpulli would offer a bondsman as a sort of collateral for the loan. And even among the hard-working Aztecs, there were some people who just did not want to face the effort and responsibility of providing their own livelihood and decided it was easier to become a slave and have someone else permanently responsible for them. Among the people who chose this kind of life were prostitutes and gamblers who felt that they wanted to trade in their risky and unsettling existence for the material security and peace of mind that slavery offered.

Such a seemingly desperate choice is made more comprehensible by the fact that slavery in Aztec society was not the grim, debilitating horror that it was in other societies at other times earlier and later in history. Aztec slaves could relate to their own families in any way they chose, could own property, could even own slaves of their own. Children of slaves were always born free. The degradation involved in slavery was primarily a social one. Slaves could not hold any civic office which, in modern terms, would be the equivalent of being deprived of all civil rights, including the right to vote. But such a stripping of civic rights was inflicted on others as well, usually as a form of punishment for committing an antisocial act that was not sufficiently severe to require criminal punishment.

Criminal punishment among the Aztecs was brutal and prompt, but it was also thoughtfully designed and meted out by a system that was carefully structured, highly efficient and, by its own standards, faultlessly just.

The judicial system began at the calpulli level. *Teuctli* (calpulli judges) were elected for one-year terms and ruled on local civil and criminal cases. The teuctli's main task was to try and settle disputes locally so that they would not jam up the higher courts. The teuctli usually passed sentence within a day or two. When this could not be done because the case was too difficult, or the crime committed too serious, the teuctli would send up the case to the next higher court, accompanied by an advisory opinion.

The next higher court was the *tecalli,* in permanent session in its own quarters of the imperial palace in Tenochtitlán. The tecalli had three members, each with a retinue of assistants to record and execute sentences. This retinue included sheriffs, scribes, policemen who served as messengers and arresting officers, and town criers, who announced the sentences both in Tenochtitlán and in the convicted person's home community.

Each province under Aztec suzerainty had a tecalli court in its own capital.

Outranking the tecalli in the judicial system was another court that doubled as a court of appeals and as a state council. It was called the *tlacxitlan* and the judge who headed it, the *cihuacotl,* was second only to the emperor himself in rank and prestige. Appeals from sentences of all the lower courts were brought to him and he ruled on them, aided by three other judges of senior rank. Their judgment was final and could not be appealed even to the emperor himself. However, the supreme justice himself could, and sometimes did, refer special cases to the emperor for a final judgment or sentence.

The tlacxitlan also met as a combination of state council and supreme court to discuss matters of high state policy and errors or offenses committed by the nobility in war or peace. In that capacity it met every ten or twelve days.

On a parallel track, there existed another high court designed to make certain that no legal case was left unsolved or delayed too long. That court met in Tenochtitlán every eighty days, with sessions lasting up to two weeks each time. Tecalli judges from each of the provinces had to attend and report on the cases they had tried and the sentences they had passed as well as on cases that were still pending. Their judgments were reviewed and difficult cases that had remained unsolved were tried and brought to a conclusion. The result of this system was that no legal case in the Aztec empire could take longer than eighty days for final adjudication.

Nobles and warriors of senior rank were judged directly by the tlacxitlan, and merchants had lower courts of their own that wrote commercial legislation and were experts in commercial conflicts. However, the court of last resort for that system, too, was the tlacxitlan.

At all levels of the judicial ladder, judges were chosen with great care. They were picked from the best graduates of the calmecac, after they had distinguished themselves through years of service in their private lives as warriors, or in other public service. They were usually men in their late thirties or forties (the Aztec, with a much shorter life span than ours, considered fifty the beginning of old age) who had built a reputation as industrious, impartial, sober and sound persons with good minds and well-controlled passions. The state compensated them with a residence, fields, and people to work the fields. They were held to strict standards. They could not accept payment of any kind from litigants; they could not sit in cases that involved relatives or friends; they could not delay cases unduly; nor pronounce judgments or issue sentences in serious or difficult cases without consulting their judicial superiors. They could themselves be sentenced for bribery, negligence, or misconduct in office, and if the misconduct in office consisted of partiality resulting in an unjust sentence, the penalty was death.

The legal procedure was sophisticated. It included the taking of oaths, and required proof, which had to be rational and consistent, in the form of confession, documents, testimony by witnesses, and cross examination.

Crimes fell into four major categories. Most frequent were crimes against other persons, involving either physical or mental assault, or damage to property. The former could range from beating up a neighbor in a quarrel to homicide, but it also included such psychological assaults as defamation, calumny, or the bearing of false witness. Property crimes ranged from robbery and abetting robbery to property damage and plundering or to abuse of confidence. The system's basic approach to such personal crimes was to aim at restitution rather than confinement. A criminal could even escape a death sentence for homicide if he could get the family of the person he killed to agree to having the murderer work it out instead.

Crimes in the other three categories were judged more harshly. Crimes against society, the second category, ranged from procuring to bad manners at the palace, from public misconduct to the unauthorized wearing of clothing or insignia. It also included disobedience to one's parents. Striking a parent was a crime that was punished by mandatory disinheritance, or death.

Crimes against authority, the third category, were punished even more quickly and severely, usually by strangling or stoning. Such crimes included refusal to pay or even negligence in paying tribute; cheating the state of revenue in any other way; stealing from the state treasury; and refusal to obey an order in peace or war.

The most heinous crimes were those in the fourth category, committed against the security of the state or the emperor himself. These included espionage, rebellion, treason and, of course, defamation of the ruler and regicide. Interestingly, it also included depriving any person unlawfully of liberty. There was, for example, a law that stipulated that any slave escaping from his master who could make his way to the grounds of the imperial palace was entitled to his freedom. Anyone apprehending such a person, or treating him like a slave in any way, was held guilty of an offense against the emperor. For crimes against the emperor or the security of the state, the punishment was not only death for the criminal but enslavement of his entire family.

The Aztec economic system also started out with communal ownership of the land, with produce divided according to need. It proliferated into a complex economic organization characterized by a substantial degree of specialization in skills and know-how, by competent use of the economics of comparative advantage, and by a wide spread in the distribution of wealth.

In the Aztecs' early days little difference existed in the way any member of Aztec society lived. Priests, warriors, and elders carried somewhat greater responsibilities than other members of society but, if anything, their existence was more austere. The responsibilities themselves were regarded as privileges.

Later those privileges became more concrete, particularly for the nobility which became a separate class as the empire grew. An impressed conquistador describes how rich Aztecs lived by the time he arrived in Mexico.

"In this city [Tenochtitlán] there were many houses belonging to the lords. They were so large and had so many rooms, and gardens on the rooftops as well as below, that they were a sight to behold. I went inside one of the houses of the great lord Montezuma more than four times for no other reason than to look at it, and each time I walked so much that I became tired, but I never saw all of it. It was the custom in all the lords' houses to have very large rooms and halls around a courtyard and in one of the houses there was a hall large enough to hold more than three thousand people comfortably."

Another conquistador, the famous Captain Bernal Díaz, was not only impressed but enchanted by the way rich Aztecs lived in his day.

"The appearance of the places in which they lodged us!" he exclaims in his diary. "How spacious and well built they are—of beautiful stonework and cedar wood, and the wood of other sweet-scented trees—with great rooms and courts covered with cotton cloth awnings, all wonderful to behold.

"Then we went to the orchard and garden, which was so wonderful to see and walk in that I was never tired of looking at the diversity of trees and noting the scent each one had, and the paths full of roses and other flowers, and the pools of fresh water. Great canoes were able to pass into the garden from the lake. And all was cemented and splendid, with many kinds of stones with pictures on them, which gave much to think about."

Was he thinking about how the Aztecs had organized their economy to make this possible? Perhaps. They were ahead of Europe in this regard. To the specialization of crafts and professions—which Europe also had—the Aztecs had added a system of community specialization based on the economics of comparative advantage. Under this system, an Aztec town located near a vein of good clay would specialize in making pottery, while a community near a salt deposit would concentrate on digging out and processing the salt. But specialization went beyond that type of relatively obvious economic logic. Some communities specialized on cultivating birds for their feathers, others on growing particularly pungent chili peppers. Some towns in the empire were known for the glossy animal skins they produced, others for their finely woven wool blankets. This concentrated exploitation of natural resources, or the equally concentrated cultivation of human resources, resulted in a society that offered a wide range of products at a level of competence rare for its day.

The Aztecs also saw to it that the products created by this system of specialization were available throughout the empire. A carefully instituted and maintained method of tribute in kind made certain that every community's resources were put at the disposal of the empire, and a complex and very well administered network of markets assured a wide distribution of goods not only in the capital but in every corner of the realm.

Each village had its permanent market and larger cities had several permanent markets. They were invariably located in the heart of the community, near the temple, which underscored their importance. In addition to these fixed centers of trade, special trade days were instituted at regular intervals, at least one each week. On these days, any person producing anything had to bring the product to the nearest market, even if this included carrying the merchandise as far as fifteen miles. And in the Aztec empire, no wheeled or animal transportation existed. Bringing goods to market meant they had to be carried there on people's backs.

The system applied to the smallest village as well as to the biggest city. Aztec markets were, in effect, the precursors of shopping centers and the goods offered were as richly varied as those displayed in a modern shopping center.

Captain Bernal Díaz describes his first visit to the main market of the Aztec capital.

"When we arrived at the great market place called Tlatelolco, we were astonished at the number of people and the quantity of merchandise and at the good order and control maintained, for we had never seen such a sight before. Each kind of merchandise was kept separate, in its own place. Let us begin with the dealers in gold, silver and precious stones, feathers, mantles and embroidered goods. Then there were Indian slaves, both men and women, and they brought them along tied to long poles, with collars round their necks so they could not escape, but others they let walk freely. Next, there were traders who sold great pieces of cotton cloth, and articles of twisted thread, and those who sold cacao. In this way one could see every type of merchandise to be found in all of New Spain. There were those who sold henequen cloth, ropes and sandals, and sweet roasted roots from this plant. In another place there were skins of tigers and lions, of otters and jackals, deer and other animals like badgers and mountain cats, some tanned and others crude, and other merchandise.

"Let us go and speak of those who sold beans and sage and other vegetables and herbs in another part, and of those who sold fowl, cocks with wattles, rabbits, deer, ducks, young dogs, and other things of that sort. Let us also mention those who sold fruit and the women who sold cooked food, dough and tripe; then every kind of pottery made in a thousand different forms, from great *ollas* to little jugs, there also had a place to themselves. Then those who sold honey and dainties like nut paste, and those who sold lumber, boards, cradles, beams, blocks and benches, each article by itself, and the vendors of pitch, and firewood. Paper, and reeds scented with liquidambar and full of tobacco, and yellow ointments, and such things are sold by themselves. Much cochineal is sold under the arcades of that great market square, and there are many vendors of herbs.

"I am forgetting those who sell salt, and those who make stone knives, and how they split them off the stone; and the fisherwomen who sell small cakes made from an ooze which they take out of the great lake which curdles, and from this they make a kind of bread with a cheese flavor. Displayed in another part are brass and copper axes and gourds, and wooden jars that are gaily painted. I wish I could tell of all the things which are sold, but they are so numerous and the great market with its porticos was so crowded with people, that one would not have been able to see and investigate everything in two days."

The good control and order of the market that so impressed Captain Díaz, along with the rich choice of merchandise, was maintained by a special contingent of inspectors and policemen. The inspectors checked daily on both quality and price of the goods offered and, if the quality was inferior or the price too high, they could confiscate the merchandise. The policemen patrolled the markets and if they saw any stealing, or if any cheating was brought to their attention, they acted immediately and harshly. An Aztec caught stealing in the marketplace could be clubbed to death on the spot. Since the markets were a vital institution in Aztec society, thieving in the market was regarded not only as a personal crime against the merchant whose goods were taken, but as a crime against society.

Most trade was in the form of barter, with one type of merchandise traded for another: a bowl of salt against a handful of chili; a feather mantle against a set of decorated jugs and plates. But some goods doubled as currencies; quills filled with gold powder; strings of copper bells and copper axes; certain shells and some precious stones, particularly jade and, most popular, what one Spanish conquistador described as "grains like almonds, called cacao." Cacao beans were the equivalent of small change in the Aztec currency system; copper products served the function of five- and ten-dollar bills; quills filled with gold dust were the counterpart to hundred-dollar notes; and jade was as rare and precious as a thousand-dollar bill.

The pioneers of this system of exchanging goods throughout the realm were the *pochteca,* the empire's merchants. Pochtecas were a separate class, with their own gods and their own courts, and special privileges which they earned by the risks they took.

They seem to have been extremely enterprising. Another famous conquistador, Bernardino de Sahagún, says:

"These merchants go over the entire land in pursuit of business, buying in one part and selling in another. There is no place where they do not seek something to buy or sell, no matter how hot or cold, nor how rough the way may be. They are daring enough to go even to enemy lands, and they are very astute at dealing with strangers, learning their languages or treating them with benevolence to attract their trade. They also know where there are skins of valuable animals and where to sell them for the best price."

Pochteca usually set out on their trading trips in sizable groups, led by an elder experienced in the world of commerce and accompanied by a retinue of apprentices and a troop of soldiers. The protection provided them by the state was reciprocated by the pochteca with services of their own, not limited to their economic role. The pochteca doubled as spies, reporting to the emperor on the terrain and social structures of the places they visited and, more ominously, on what new provinces might be worth conquering for the tribute they would bring. In their travels, the pochteca were sometimes attacked by enemies of the Aztec empire or by people who just did not want them in their midst. And sometimes the pochtecas deliberately provoked attack. Whatever the reason for the attack, an assault on a group of pochtecas minding their business was considered by the emperor to be sufficient cause for war. Peacefully or belligerently, wherever the pochteca went, the Aztec flag sooner or later followed.

CHAPTER SEVEN

All that Our Hearts Desire . . .

IS Death in War. This sentence describes precisely how the Aztecs felt about fighting. It is the last line of a poem that celebrates one of the central passions of Aztec society, the mystic love of death. It illustrates the fundamental perversity that had crept into Aztec civilization and explains what made the Aztecs such formidable conquerors.

The poem—the song of a soldier facing a day of battle—reads:

Bells clamor
The chieftain is resplendent
He who makes the world is full of delight.
The shield flowers are opening their petals.
Glory spreads

Revolves about the earth.
Here is the intoxication of death in the heart of the plain!
Here, as war bursts upon the plain,
The chieftain shines, spins, whirls
In the flowery death of war.
Oh Princes!
Oh Aztec chieftains!
Fear not, my heart:
On the plain
I covet death by the obsidian knife.
All that our hearts desire
Is death in war.

The love of death felt by this soldier was not a personal aberration. It was the natural result of values taught by the priests of the Aztecs' chief deity, the tribal firegod Huitzilopochtli, reinforced by social rewards of wealth and status, and inculcated in Aztec babies from the day they were born.

There exists in Aztec mythology a divine message that was to the Aztecs the equivalent of the Ten Commandments. The message came directly from Huitzilopochtli and, in an intriguing historic parallel, was conveyed to the Aztecs during their migration from the lonely island of the wild cranes to the promised land that became Tenochtitlán. The Huitzilopochtli message is, however, not a set of theological and ethical injunctions. It is the description of a mission and the rewards that come with carrying it out. It reads:

"Behold, Aztecas! Here is your responsibility and your vocation.

"From all four corners of the earth, you are to conquer, earn, and subdue for yourselves.

"Have then body, breast, head, arms, and strength, for it will cost much sweat, work and pure blood for you to ob-

tain and enjoy the fine emeralds, precious stones, gold, silver, fine feather-work, rare feathers of all colors, fine chocolate brought from afar, cotton of different hues, many sweet-smelling flowers, all manners of different, delicious, delicate fruits, and many other things bringing great pleasure and contentment."

Just how effective this martial evangelism proved in molding the Aztec mind is illustrated by an Aztec knight, a member of the elite corps of the Eagle Knights, who describes what his life is about. He states it simply, with no feelings of guilt or remorse, or, for that matter, of pride or glory. The knight says:

"I was sent on this mission, and I was charged to bring arms, bow, arrows, and shield. My principal purpose in coming is war, and likewise with my breast, my head, and in my arms I must look after and carry on my vocation in many cities and among the people there are today.

"First, I shall conquer in war in order to have and name my home of precious emerald and gold, decorated with feather-work. The house shall be adorned with precious emerald as transparent as crystal, and I shall have all kinds of precious heads of corn, chocolate, cotton, and cloth of many colors. And I shall have it all to see and to possess, for it is commanded of me and my office and for that purpose I came."

This total, almost negligent acceptance of rapacious greed is not surprising in a culture in which male children were taught before they could even understand the words that the true purpose of their life was to supply the gods with blood—their own and that of friends and enemies—and that their real existence was not on this earth but, after death in war, in their true home, the house of their celestial ancestor, the sun.

When an Aztec boy was born, his first cries were not answered by a pacifier but by the traditional, and presumably soothing words of the midwife who crooned to the infant:

"My deeply loved and tender son. Here is the word that

was given to us by the gods. This place where you were just born is not your true house, because you are a soldier and servant of the gods. Your land is not here but in another place. You are promised to the field of battle, and your talents and abilities will be dedicated to war. Your obligation is to give to the sun the blood of your enemies to drink, and to feed the earth with the corpses of your opponents. Your own land, your inheritance, and your fortune is the house of the sun. There you will serve, and rejoice in his service, if by some happy fortune you are worthy of dying by the flowery death."

"The flowery death" was death in war. It was such a passionate addiction among the Aztecs that, even when they were not fighting for territory or tribute, they arranged for what they called "flower wars." The pretty name is misleading. These engagements were not fought with flowers. They were a deadly escalation of the jousts that served an analogous purpose in medieval Europe. In Europe, knights displayed their skill and valor on festive occasions in which, occasionally, someone got hurt or even died. In the Aztecs' "flower wars," the flowers were weapons and the festivities called for thousands of lives to be snuffed out so their blood could be poured on the altars of Huitzilopochtli, to delight him and his fellow deities.

Since every Aztec boy was, in fact, born and raised to become a soldier, the Aztec army was a citizens' militia, reflecting Aztec society in its organization, its inspiration, its order, and its justice. Priests led Aztec forces in battle, blessing and urging on the combatants in the morning before the fighting began and at dusk when the prisoners were brought in. Military courts functioned in the field and in the capital. In the field they ruled on such immediate but relatively minor matters as who, of two contesting soldiers, could rightfully claim a particular prisoner. In Tenochtitlán, where the military tribunal sat in the emperor's palace, it decided on such important issues as acts of treason or cowardice, the betrayal of battle plans to the enemy, or the even more heinous crime of displaying fear in battle or attempting to run away. Such behavior carried the death penalty since it was vital to the Aztec way of life that no soldier capable of cowardice should survive to contaminate the army.

The Aztec military ethos was also upheld by the fact that an Aztec soldier in battle was surrounded by his neighbors. As a citizens' army, Aztec military organization duplicated the model of civilian life. The Aztecs fought in clans, in units of 20. These basic units were subdivisions of units of 200 and 400, which represented hamlets, villages, and towns. The men who commanded Aztec soldiers in battle were the same men who ruled them in civilian life. In the Aztec army, men who fought together knew each other intimately and, perhaps even more important, knew that they would spend the rest of their lives in close proximity. There was no escape. The way a man performed in battle would earn him respect or contempt, not only from his rulers and his peers, but also from his immediate neighbors for as long as he lived.

Aztecs fought in civilian garments, adding only weapons, headdress, and insignia. Aztec weapons ranged from bow and arrow to the famous *atlatl,* a spear-thrower that was the Aztecs' long-distance weapon. For close-in fighting the Aztecs used wooden clubs with blades of finely honed obsidian, and they carried shields that were decorative as well as protective. The shields were made of wicker covered with hide, and the hide was either dramatically painted or covered with glowing featherwork. Aztec soldiers also wore suits of armor made of quilted cotton soaked in brine which covered the entire body. Impregnated with the salt solution, the garment must have been both stiff and scratchy but the Spaniards understandably thought it a great improvement, for both mobility and comfort, over their own steel armor.

What really distinguished a man in the Aztec army was his headdress and his insignia. Aztec knights and chiefs

Aztec armor was made of quilted cotton, soaked in brine. It was not quite as effective as the steel armor of the conquistadors, but it was easier to wear.

wore wooden helmets, elaborately carved and decorated to resemble the heads of powerful real or mythical animals: jaguars and eagles, pumas and feathered serpents. They carried their insignia on their backs, and it ranged from a handful of tall feathers indicating a clan to immense wooden structures, covered with featherwork and jewelry. Since the size and richness of this insignia was directly proportionate to a soldier's valor and repute, perhaps the mere sight of it was enough to frighten opponents. Certainly, the helmets, shields, and insignia made the Aztec army a colorful force.

Aztec tactics were limited by logistical constraints. The Aztec army did not live off the land. It brought along its own provisions which consisted of every soldier carrying a bag of food and drink on his back. This meant that battles could not last long and indeed they did not. The Aztec army fought from dawn to dusk, for one day when an engagement went well, for three days when a battle was hard. Leading the Aztec force were the priests. They were followed by a group of knights and specially chosen commanders. The main body of the army followed, and fought in relays.

When the Aztec army marched to battle, it did so in silence. But once fighting began, whoops and yells, and the sound of drums and whistles became an important part of the fighting, serving as a kind of emotional/psychological arsenal.

A battle was won when the enemy fled or surrendered, or when the opponents' commander was captured. If none of these occurred, victory was established by Aztec forces successfully assaulting the temple of the enemy, which they invariably set on fire. Characteristically, the Aztec ideogram for victory is a burning temple, sometimes a burning temple with a spear running through it.

The outcome of an engagement was relayed immediately to Tenochtitlán. A military messenger was dispatched as soon as the battle was over, and his appearance conveyed at a glance what had happened. If he entered Tenochtitlán with his mantle tied over his body in the customary man-

ner, this indicated that nothing much had occurred, that the outcome of the engagement had been either indecisive or unimportant. If the Aztec army had suffered defeat—a rare occurrence—the messenger arrived in the temple on the main square of Tenochtitlán with his hair hanging loose to cover his face, and in deadly silence. On the more frequent occasions when the messenger came to report another victory, his hair was neatly braided and he brandished a club and a decorated shield. When the people saw that always welcome sight, they left their labors, strewed the roads with flowers, and thronged the causeways to greet the returning army with music and incense. A victorious Aztec army came home to a delirious welcome.

What did the Aztec military machine look like to the Spaniards who, with their horses and muskets, their steel helmets and coats of mail, were of course infinitely better equipped for welfare? The Spaniards, it appears, were dazzled and impressed. The famous anonymous conquistador to whose observations we owe so much detail of Aztec life at the time of the conquest summarizes his impression of the Aztecs' organization.

"They have their military system, for they have captains general, and also captains of four hundred and two hundred men. Each company has its standard bearer with the insignia on a staff tied to his back in such a way that it neither hinders him in fighting nor in doing whatever he wishes, and it is so securely bound to his body that it cannot be untied or taken from him unless his body is cut to pieces.

"It is their custom to reward a man very highly, who serves well in war or performs some outstanding feat. Even though he may be the lowest slave among them, they make him a captain and lord, giving him vassals and honoring him."

Reporting on how the Aztecs equip themselves for warfare and conduct themselves in battle, the conquistador writes:

"The armor they use are shirts, like jumpers, of quilted

The face of an Aztec warrior. This man was a member of the elite corps of the Eagle knights.

cotton the thickness of a finger and a half and sometimes two fingers, which is very strong. Over these they wear suits all of one piece and of a heavy cloth, which they tie in back. These are covered with feathers and different colors and look very jaunty. One company of soldiers will wear them in red and white, another in blue and yellow, and others in various ways.

"The lords wear certain smock-like coats which among us are of mail but theirs are of gold or gilt silver, and the strength of their feathered garments is proportionate to their weapons, so that they resist spears and arrows, and even the sword. To defend the head, they wear things like heads of serpents, or tigers, or lions or wolves, and the man's head lies inside the animal's jaws as though it were devouring him. These heads are of wood covered on the outside with feathers or incrustations of gold and precious stones, and are something wonderful to see.

"They carry shields of various kinds made of strong solid cane woven with heavy double cotton, and decorated with feathers and round plaques of gold. The shields are so strong that only a good crossbow can shoot through them, but arrows do not damage them.

"The offensive arms are bows and arrows, and spears which they throw with crossbows made of another pole. The spearheads are of hard stone, or a fishbone that is very strong and sharp, and some spears have three points. Their maces have three points inserted in the same manner, so that in one thrust they produce three wounds. They have swords that are like broadswords, but their hilts are not quite so long and are three fingers wide; they are made of wood with grooves into which they fit hard stone blades which cut like a Tolosa blade. One day an Indian I saw in combat with a mounted horseman struck the horse in the chest, cutting through to the inside and killing the horse on the spot. On the same day I saw another Indian give a horse a sword thrust in the neck that laid the horse dead at his feet.

"They have slings with which they shoot very far, and many if not most of the warriors carry all these kinds of weapons in combat. It is one of the most beautiful sights in the world to see them in their battle array because they keep formation wonderfully and are very handsome. Among them are extraordinarily brave men who face death with absolute determination. I saw one of them defend himself courageously against two swift horses, and another against three and four and, when the Spanish horsemen could not kill him, one of the horsemen in desperation hurled his lance, which the Indian caught in the air and fought with for more than an hour, until two foot soldiers approached and wounded him with two or three arrows. He turned on one of the soldiers but the other grasped him from behind and stabbed him."

Not particularly inclined toward gentleness and mercy in warfare themselves, the conquistadors nevertheless found the Aztecs ferocious even by Spanish soldiers' own atrocious standards. The anonymous conquistador observes:

"During combat they sing and dance and sometimes give the wildest shouts and whistles imaginable, especially when they know they have the advantage. Anyone facing them for the first time can be terrified by their screams and their ferocity. In warfare they are the most cruel people to be found, for they spare neither brothers, relatives, friends, nor women even if they are beautiful. They kill them all. When they cannot take the enemy plunder and booty with them, they burn everything."

CHAPTER NINE

Tenochtitlán Tumbles

THE Spaniards first set foot on the Aztec Empire in the spring of 1519. Coming from Cuba, 560 men in 13 ships, they landed on Mexico's east coast in the port now called Veracruz.

Two and a half years later, Tenochtitlán fell, seven-eighths of it reduced to rubble and ashes. The Aztec dead numbered in excess of 120,000 and a comparable number, starving, homeless and dazed, straggled out of the corpse of the capital to find sustenance and solace in the countryside.

On August 13, 1521, the Spaniards celebrated their victory. It was a sultry, rain-drenched night, wrapped in a deathly silence, reports conquistador Bernal Díaz, by then a captain in the army of Cortés who had fought all the way from the coast to the capital and was on hand for the celebration. It did not give him much joy.

"There was thunder and lightning that evening," he says, "and up until midnight it rained harder than it had done before that year . . .

"All of us soldiers were as deaf as though up to now we had been in a bell tower with all the bells ringing. For the ninety-three days of the siege [of Tenochtitlán], there had been constant cries and whistles day and night, the shouts of Mexican captains giving orders on the causeways, others crying to the canoes, putting up palisades, and making barricades. In addition to all this their accursed drums and horns never stopped sounding from their towers and oratories, so that it was impossible to hear anyone talk. Now . . . all the noise and voices had stopped . . .

"Cortés ordered a banquet to celebrate. A ship had arrived from Castile with a cargo of wine, and a supply of hogs had come from Cuba. All the captains and the soldiers who had distinguished themselves from our three camps were invited, but when we went to dine there were not enough tables and chairs for a third of us, which caused great confusion. In fact, for many reasons it would have been better if the banquet had not been given.

"The plant of Noah [wine] caused some men to do foolish things. Men walked on the tables and afterward couldn't manage to make their way to the patio. Others said they were going to buy horses with gold saddles. Crossbowmen talked of arrows and quivers of gold. Others rolled down the steps. After the tables were taken away, what ladies there were danced with the younger men loaded down with their cotton padding. It struck me as a scene that was completely ridiculous."

But there was another aspect to the Spaniards and their conquests that manifested itself the morning following when the conquistadors celebrated a high mass, offering thanks on their knees, with heads bowed, for their victory.

The events of the conquest were intensely dramatic, and had the fateful inevitability of true tragedy. The main actors were complex, fascinating men and women, who reflected in their own characters the essence of the Spanish-Aztec encounter: A desire, on both sides, to understand the other, and the devastating inability to translate that desire into reality.

This struggle to comprehend the mind and spirit, goals and aspirations of another people makes the final chapter of the Aztec story a very modern tale with echoes that have already reverberated through nearly half a millennium of history. The fall of the Aztecs, and the implications of that fall, turn out to be more lasting and meaningful to mankind than their brief and brilliant rise.

The conquest of Mexico began on a stretch of tropical coast on the country's easternmost shores which was at the time part of the territory of the Totonacs. The Totonacs were what today we would call a pragmatic people. They had fallen prey to Aztec hegemony and paid tribute to Tenochtitlán. They did not like either of these two arrangements, but since they were far away from the Aztecs' capital on the inland lake, the political bonds were lax and bearable. The Totonacs were in fact governed by their own chiefs and elders.

The Totonacs teamed up with the Spaniards almost as soon as they had landed. The reason for this alliance was not only the Totonacs' disenchantment with Tenochtitlán, but also the judgment, after a couple of skirmishes with the conquistadors and a sober view of Spanish ships, horses, and arms, that these powerful people with their powerful weapons could not be beaten, and that it was therefore the better part of discretion to join them. The great contribution made by the Totonacs to the conquistadors, however, was not the quick acquiescence to Spanish might, but the discovery, and presentation to the Spaniards, of the one person who was probably as instrumental in the conquest of the Aztecs as Cortés himself. That person was Marina, the woman from Tabasco, who served as Cortès's interpreter throughout the conquest. The Indians called her Malinche, the Aztec word for tongue. Her importance is illuminated by the fact that the Aztecs called Cortés himself not by his own name but referred to him as Malintzin, which means Malinche's master.

As the Spaniards marched inland from the coast, they picked up other allies. The most important in military terms were the Tlaxcalans, who fought with the Spaniards to Tenochtitlán and beyond, and participated in each segment of the Spanish conquest. The Tlaxcalans were symptomatic of the soft underbelly of the Aztecs' tough empire. They hated the conquerors from Tenochtitlán, had chafed under the Aztec yoke from the moment it was imposed on them, and happily took the first opportunity to shake it off.

Closer to Tenochtitlán itself, the Spaniards picked up another valuable ally: Texcoco. The Texcocans had preceded the Aztecs on the shores of the lake that constituted the heart of the Aztec Empire. It was, in fact, called Lake Texcoco for the very good reason that the Texcocans were an established, advanced community when the Aztecs arrived as ragamuffin nomads from the north. The Texcocan court was already a center of poetry and philosophy at the time the Aztecs were dedicating all their energies to the ruthless grab for empire. Even though the Texcocans finally wound up under Aztec suzerainty themselves, they never ceased to regard themselves as the older, superior civilization and the Aztecs as arrogant upstarts. They had no objection, therefore, to helping anyone who could dish out to the Aztecs some of their own bitter medicine.

On the other side of the encounter, the Spaniards displayed the dynamic strength as well as the enervating weakness of their system and values.

The conquistadors quarreled among themselves frequently and bitterly and jockeyed unceasingly for the best position to get their hands on gold in this rich new world, and the best vantage point from which to enhance their reputations at the faraway court of Castile. In these internecine maneuverings they were as unscrupulous as they were pretentious. They combined guile, calumny, and callousness with fawning pronouncements about love, loyalty, and devotion. At one point in Cortés's conquest of Mexico, the quarreling among the Spaniards got so bad and the morale of the conquistadors fell so low that Cortés burned his own ships in order to prevent his captains and troops from quitting the conquest and returning to the relative peace and comforts of Cuba, where the Spaniards had already established a quite luxurious society on the economic underpinnings of a plantation culture worked with slaves.

As the Spaniards marched inland, astonishment and admiration abounded on both sides. The Aztecs were impressed by the martial accomplishments of the Spaniards, and by their competence and courage. They never got over their awe at the Spaniards' appearance: their pale skins, their beards, their iron helmets, their armor, their velvet breeches, and of course their horses, a novel apparition in the Americas. So novel that at first the Aztecs believed horse and rider to be one creature and probably divine.

The Spaniards for their part were incredulous at the advanced civilization they met: the houses, the temples, the floating gardens, the profuse, well-organized markets, the rich appointments of palaces, the elaborate attire of nobles, the fastidiousness of Aztec manners and the Aztec way of life as they encountered it at the top level of Aztec society.

The fascination, the desire to understand and to deal with each other peacefully—and the tragic failure to do so—is illustrated most poignantly by the first encounter of Cortés, by then unquestioned leader of the Spaniards in Mexico, and Montezuma, reigning head of the Aztec Empire.

Montezuma and Cortés met on November 8, 1519, when the Spaniards were still quite some distance from Tenochtitlán. Montezuma had tried in a number of ways to dissuade the conquistadors from marching on his capital and the personal meeting with Cortés was his final attempt to achieve this aim peacefully. He was carried to the meeting in a splendid litter from which he descended to greet Cortés face to face. Cortés wanted to embrace him, in the Spanish fashion. The nobles attending Montezuma quickly made clear that an embrace was not welcome, because no one was permitted to touch the person of the emperor. Montezuma attempted to signal his friendship with the symbolic greeting of touching his hand to the ground, then bringing it to his heart and head. To the Aztec emperor this meant: "You stand in my realm and my heart and mind welcome you." No one knows how Cortés interpreted the gesture, but the chances are that he thought it a deep bow indicating, however subtly and imperiously, submission. He was, of course, wrong.

Bernal Díaz, the redoubtable captain and chronicler who fought with Cortés from the very beginning to the very end and managed to record everything of importance or interest along the way, describes that first encounter:

"The great Montezuma approached in a rich litter, accompanied by other great lords and chiefs . . . Montezuma descended from his litter while these great chiefs supported him with their arms beneath a marvelously rich canopy of green feathers, worked with gold and silver, pearls and *chalchiuis* [precious and semiprecious stones used by the Aztecs as jewelry], which hung from a kind of border that was wonderful to see. He was richly dressed and wore shoes like sandals, with soles of gold covered with precious stones. The four chiefs who supported him were also richly dressed, in clothes that had apparently been held ready for them on the road, for they had not worn them when they received us earlier. There were four other chiefs who carried the canopy and many other lords who walked before the great Montezuma, sweeping the ground where he would pass, and putting down mats so that he would not have to walk on the ground. None of these lords looked in his face; all of them kept their eyes down, with great reverence.

"When Cortés saw the great Montezuma approaching, he jumped from his horse and they showed great respect toward each other."

But beneath the respect there was fear and distrust and, most important, a mutual misunderstanding of motives and actions. The initial courtesies soon exploded into confrontations and those confrontations flared into open and bitter war. It was a see-saw war that lasted for the better part of a year and a half. What enraged the Aztecs most in the course of the clash was a gratuitous massacre perpetrated on the people of Tenochtitlán by one of Cortés's more brutal and reckless captains, Pedro de Alvarado, who later choked the civilization of the Maya in a sea of blood.

For the Spaniards, the most devastating event was what became known in the annals of the conquistadors as the *noche triste,* the sad night, when the Spaniards decided to withdraw from Tenochtitlán and found that the Aztecs had burned the bridges and breached the causeways that led out of the city. In their desperate attempt to escape, the Spaniards found themselves climbing over corpses, their own as well as those of the Aztecs, to get out. More shattering still from their vantage point, they had to use long-hoarded treasure, including caskets stuffed with gold and the bodies of horses, alive and dead, to construct pontoons of a kind to help them flee across the water from the fury of the Aztecs who, by then, were determined to exterminate every Spaniard they could capture.

The slaughter that night was such that Cortés, famous for his cool and calculating nature even under the greatest stress, broke down and wept. The cypress tree under which he reportedly shed his tears still exists and today's Mexicans regard it with much the same feeling that citizens of the United States of America have for Valley Forge.

After a while, the Spaniards rallied from the rout of the sad night and began to lay siege to Tenochtitlán. The siege lasted eighty days. At the end, a sick and starving people concentrated its last resistance in the great twin temples in the heart of the city. When these finally went up in flames, Tenochtitlán surrendered. The Aztec empire had come to an end.

The eagle was the core symbol of the Aztecs and remains the symbol of the people of Mexico. This is an Aztec eagle carved on wood.

To understand the tragic events of these two historic years in the annals of the Americas one must know what went on in the hearts and minds of the two peoples that found themselves pitted against each other in a consuming fury when they had hoped, each in its way, to turn their initial awe and admiration of each other into a human bond that would last.

We have historic records from both sides that make such an understanding possible.

How the Aztecs perceived the Spaniards and what the conquistadors meant in the history of Montezuma and his people, becomes clear by studying one of the Aztec codices that have survived. These codices were written in the first or second generation after the conquest. They are based on oral transmissions of events and are illustrated by Aztec artists. The account that follows comes from the Codex Florentino and tells, first, of the report that was brought to Montezuma from messengers he sent to the coast when he first heard of the landing of Cortés at Veracruz. Not surprisingly, these messengers were baffled and awed by the Spaniards' strange faces and clothes, but even more by their horses and cannons, neither of which they had seen before. They thought that the horses were either a tall species of deer, or giant dogs, and that the cannons were a kind of black magic. And they believed that the bread the Spaniards ate was human flesh.

As the Codex Florentino puts it:

"When he heard what those who were sent had to tell, he [Montezuma] was amazed and struck with wonder . . .

"It caused him great wonder to hear how the cannon fires, how the noise resounds, and how because of this a person can faint, how this confuses a person's ears. And how, when the shot falls, something like a stone comes out from its inside, how it rains fire, sparks fall. And the smoke which comes from it, very noxious; it smells like putrid mud, it enters the head and is very disturbing.

"Then if it strikes against a hill, as it did, it breaks a hole, it splits the hill open; and if it strikes against a tree it breaks that into splinters as if it were a portent, as if someone had blown from the inside.

"Their war equipment is all of iron. Their dress is iron, something like a helmet of iron they put on their heads, their swords are iron, their arrows, their shields; iron are their spears.

"They are carried on the backs of their 'deer.' These are as high as roofs.

"All parts of the bodies of the men of Castile are covered, only their faces appear. They are white, as if they were made of lime. They have yellow hair, but some have black. Long are their beards, also yellow; and their mustaches are yellow. Their hair is fine and a little wavy.

"As for their food, it is human nourishment. They eat much; it is white, not heavy, as if it were straw, wood of the maize stalk, and the taste is like the inside of the maize stalk: a little sweet, a little as if it was besmeared with honey. It is eaten like honey; it is sweet food.

"Then, their dogs are enormous, with ears hanging down and close to the head, with long tongues hanging out. They have eyes which shoot out fire, throw out sparks. Their eyes are yellow, a deep yellow. Their bellies are proud, distended like a ribbed framework. They are very stout and strong. They are not peaceful, they go panting, with their tongues hanging out. They are marked the color of tigers, with many colored spots."

Not surprisingly, the Codex Florentino says, "When he had heard all this, Montezuma was filled with terror, as if his heart had contracted, as if his heart had swooned. He was overcome with anguish."

Montezuma's anguish was in part caused by the fact that in his secret heart he was convinced that the Spaniards had come to fulfill a prophecy, that Cortés was the god-teacher Quetzalcoatl returned in human form to rule the people of Mexico as he had done in the old, golden age of Teotihuacán. Montezuma believed that he was yielding his throne and his empire to a god. The belief created confusion in his mind and chaos in his heart.

Montezuma's inner conviction and confusion emerges in his first encounter with Cortés. Alighting from his litter, he greets the conquistador who has dismounted from his horse and says:

"My lord, you are weary, you are tired. But now you have come to your land. You have arrived at your city, Mexico. Here you have come to sit upon your throne. Oh, for a brief time they have kept it for you, they have preserved it, those who have gone away, those who were taking your place . . . Oh, for what a brief time did they care for it in your name, did they rule over the city of Mexico. The common people were cared for under their shoulders, under their power.

"Do they see, perhaps know, those they left, those who stayed behind? Oh, may one of them be watching and see with amazement what I now see in front of me! What now I see, I, the remaining one, the survivor of our lords. No, no, I am not dreaming. I did not get up from the ground still sleeping. I do not see it in dreams, I am not dreaming . . .

"It is indeed you that I have seen. My eyes have rested on your face! For five days, for ten days I have been in agony. My gaze has been fixed on the region of mystery. And you have come from among the clouds, from within the mist. Just as it was left recorded by the kings, by those who reigned, those who governed your city, that you would come to install yourself in your place, your seat of honor. That you would come here . . .

"So now it has happened. Now you are here. With great fatigue, with great effort you have come. You have arrived in your land. Come now and rest. Take possession of your royal houses. Refresh your body. Be in your land, my lord."

Cortés reacted to this astonishing welcome with courtesy, perhaps even with good will. It is hard to tell with Cortés. He was an adroit diplomat and what he said did not always reflect his intent.

On this momentous occasion he responded with reassuring grace.

"Be reassured Montezuma," Cortés said. "Have no fear. We have great affection for you. Today our hearts are at peace. We see your face. We hear you. For a long time now we have wanted to see you.

"Now we have come. Now we have arrived at your house in Mexico. In this way, therefore, you can hear our words now with complete tranquillity."

But the promised tranquillity was brief. Very shortly after they had entered Tenochtitlán, the Spaniards made Montezuma a prisoner in his palace and the clash of wills and arms was on. The all-out battle began while Cortés was away from the city, and the reckless and cruel Pedro de Alvarado launched a massacre of the citizens of Tenochtitlán as they were celebrating a holy day.

An Aztec account describes the event:

"Thus it happened. While they [the people of Tenochtitlán] were enjoying the feast, while there was dancing, there was singing, already one song was entwined with another and the songs were as the uproar of waves, at this precise moment the men of Castile decided to kill the people. They came on foot, carrying their shields of metal and their swords.

"Quickly they came up to those who were dancing. They rushed to the place of the drums. They struck at the one who was playing the drums. They cut off both his arms. Then they chopped off his head and it fell far away.

"In a moment they were clashing at them. They were running their spears through the people and hacking them. With the swords they wounded them. Some they attacked from behind and immediately these fell to the ground with their entrails hanging out. Others they severed the head and then chopped it into small pieces.

"Others they struck on the shoulders, made gashes in them. Their bodies remained mutilated. Some they wounded in the thigh, some in the calf, others straight in the abdomen, and all their entrails fell to the ground.

"There were some who tried in vain to run away. They were dragging their intestines and their feet became entangled in them. Anxious to save themselves, they found no place to go.

"Some tried to get out. There at the entrance, they were stabbed, they were cut down. Some scaled the walls. But they could not save themselves. Others went into the communal houses. There they were safe for a while. Others lay among the dead. In order to escape they pretended to be dead. By appearing to be dead, they were safe. But if anyone got up on his feet, they saw it and they cut him down.

"The blood of the warriors ran as if it were water, like water which makes little pools. The stench of blood filled the air, and the stench of the entrails which seemed to crawl along by themselves.

"And the men of Castile went everywhere, even searching the communal houses. Everywhere they thrust their weapons, looking to see if someone was hidden there. Everywhere they probed, they pried into everything."

After that, neither understanding nor peace were possible anymore. And when it was all over, when splendid Tenochtitlán had gone up in flame and the Aztec empire turned to ashes, an Aztec poet looked back at the sequence of events and sadly sang:

All this happened to us.
We saw it.
We marveled at it.
With this sad and mournful destiny
We saw ourselves afflicted.
On the roads lie broken arrows
Our hair is in disarray.

Without roofs are the houses
And red are their walls with blood.

Worms multiply in the streets and squares
And on the walls brains are spattered.
Red are the waters as if they were dyed
And when we drink
The water tastes bitter.

We struggled against the walls of adobe
But our heritage was a net made of holes.
Our shields were our protection
But not even with shields could we defend
ourselves.

We have eaten branches of linnet
We have chewed the salty grass
Bits of adobe and ground earth
Small lizards, rats, worms.
We ate meat
When it was scarcely on the fire.
When the meat was cooked
We snatched it out of the very coals
And ate it.

They put a price on us.
The price for a young person, for a priest,
A child or a young girl.
And it was enough.
For a common man
The price was only two handfuls of corn
Or ten portions of caked mosquitoes.
Our price was only
Twenty portions of salty grass.

Gold, jade, rich mantles,
Plumage of the quetzal,
All that has value
Was then counted as nothing.

The Aztec poet's elegy tells much about the way the Aztecs saw the Spaniards. And how did the Spaniards see the Aztecs? Many conquistador accounts describe the astonishment the Spaniards felt at the accomplishments they encountered. But as many tell of the disgust and horror the conquistadors felt at the Aztec mode of worship. One ranking conquistador, Andrés de Tapia, recorded his first visit to an Aztec temple, including his first vision of an Aztec skull rack. The account is disciplined and factual, but the tremor of terror emerges beneath and between the lines.

Thus, Andrés de Tapia:

"The courtyard of the idols was so large that there would be space enough for the houses of four hundred Spanish people. In its center was a tower with one hundred and thirteen steps of more than a span each, and this was solid. At the top were two rooms, higher than a pike and a half, and here was the principal god of all the land. He was made from all kinds of seeds, which had been ground and kneaded with the blood of virgin boys and girls. These they had killed by cutting open their breasts and taking out the heart, and from there they took the blood and kneaded it with the seeds into a mass thicker than a man and as high. At the time of their feasts they adorned the figure with the kind of gold jewelry they wore when they dressed for great festivals. They wrapped the figure in very thin mantles, making a bundle. Then, with many ceremonies, they made a beverage and put it with this figure inside the room at the top of the tower. They also gave some of this beverage to the one they elected captain-general when there was a war, or something of great importance. They put these things between the outer wall of the tower and another inner wall, leaving no opening so that it seemed there was nothing there.

"Outside the hollow wall were two idols on large stone bases the height of a measuring rod. The idols were nearly the height of three measuring rods, and the girth of an ox. They were of polished granite covered with mother-of-pearl, which is the shell that the pearl grows in. Over this they used a glue in the form of a paste to incrust gold ornamentation, and designs of men, serpents, birds, and other figures made of large and small turquoises, emeralds, and amethysts, so that all of the mother-of-pearl was covered except in some places where they left it to make a design with the stones. These idols wore thick gold serpents, and for necklaces some ten or twelve human hearts made of gold. For faces they had gold masks with mirror eyes, and at the nape of the neck hung another face like a human head without flesh.

"There were more than five thousand men in the service of this idol, some of them superior to the rest in rank as well as dress. They had their high priest whom they devoutly obeyed, and whom Montezuma as well as all the other lords held in great veneration. They arose promptly at midnight for their sacrifice, which was the letting of blood from the tongue and the arms and thighs—sometimes from one place and sometimes from another—and wetting straws in the blood and offering them before an enormous oakwood fire. Then they went out to the idol tower to offer incense.

"At a crossbow's throw from this tower, and facing it, were sixty or seventy very tall beams set on a platform made of stone and mortar. Lining the platform steps were many skulls set in mortar, with their teeth bared. At each end of the row of beams was a tower made of mortar and skulls with bared teeth, apparently built without any other stones. The beams were a little less than a measuring rod apart, and from top to bottom as many poles as there were room for had been fitted across, each pole holding five skulls pierced through the temples. The one who writes this, together with Gonzalo de Umbria, counted the poles and multiplied them by the five skulls hung between beams, and found there were 136,000 skulls, not counting the ones on the towers."

When the Spaniards encountered their first Aztec warriors they were as shocked and demoralized by what they saw and heard as were the Aztecs when they first came upon the conquistadors' steeds and cannons.

Conquistador Francisco de Aguilar describes the Spaniards' first view of the warriors of Tlaxcala.

"Here, over seven or eight leagues of plains, we could see many towns and temples of the kind the Indians build, and on these plains we also saw and met countless numbers of warriors who were very well armed in their fashion. They use a cotton armor, cudgels and swords, and a great many bows and arrows. Many of them carried standards and gold shields, and other insignia which they wore strapped to their backs, giving them an appearance of great ferocity, since they also had their faces stained, and grimaced horribly, giving great leaps and shouts and cries. These put such fear into us that many of the Spaniards asked for confession."

Aguilar also reports in detail what happened during the *noche triste,* the sad night when the Spaniards withdrew from Tenochtitlán in an agony of confusion before they rallied for the final siege and conquest.

Here is Aguilar's account:

"As night set in, Captain Hernando Cortés and the other captains gave orders for everyone to leave quietly. However, these preparations were not enough nor was it even possible, because of the brightness of the moon and the lighted braziers in the streets and on the rooftops, to leave without being seen. Many of the Christians were wounded, and provision was made for each of the few horses to carry two or three of them, which meant that there were barely enough horses for all of them. While this was going on a windstorm had risen, so that by nine or ten o'clock it was thundering and hailing as if the heavens were bursting. Rather than a natural thing, it seemed truly that God wished to work a miracle to save us, for it was not possible that all of us should be left there that night to die.

"When we had crossed the canals and silently reached the

end of the causeway, an Indian who was on guard there dropped into the canal and climbed to a nearby roof, and began to shout loudly: 'O valiant men of Mexico: What are you doing, that these whom we had ready to kill are getting away from us?' And this he said over and over again. During the tempest and hailstorm I have mentioned, the Indian warriors and sentries had come in out of the downpour and gone to sleep; but we Spaniards put up with any hardships to save our lives. As soon as this sentry gave the alarm, they all ran out with their weapons to cut us off, following us with great fury, shooting arrows, spears and stones, and wounding us with their swords. Here many Spaniards fell, some dead and some wounded, and others without any injury who fainted away from fright. And since all of us were fleeing, there was not a man who would lift a hand to help his companion or even his own father, nor a brother his own brother.

"It happened that certain Spanish cavaliers and hildagos, about forty in all, and most of them horsemen and brave men, were carrying out a great amount of baggage. Captain Cortés's aide, who rode with them, also carried a large amount. Since these Spaniards had to go slowly, the Mexicans, who were the bravest of warriors, blocked their way and forced them back to the courtyards, where they fought with them three days and nights. The Spaniards defended themselves valiantly from the tops of the towers; nevertheless, due to hunger and the swarms of people gathered there against them, they were wiped out.

"As we were fleeing it was heartbreaking to see our companions dying, and to see how the Indians carried them off to tear them to pieces. The number of Indians pursuing us could have been about five or six thousand, because the rest of the horde of warriors were occupied in looting the baggage that had sunk in the canals. They were even cutting one another's hands off to get a larger amount of the plunder. And so it happened that God miraculously provided that the baggage, and those who carried it, and the forty men who were left behind, saved us from all being killed and torn to pieces.

"It took us from midnight to the night of the following day to reach the Tower of Victory, now called Nuestra Señora de los Remedios, which is half a league away, or a league and a half from the point where we left. On the following morning, after review of the troops, we found that more than half of our army had been killed. The rest of us, nearly starved, began the painful march toward Tlaxcala."

The Spaniards triumphed in the end, not because their weapons or martial skills were superior. They won because the Aztecs, even when driven to the utmost extremity by the conquistadors, were beset by a gnawing faith that these men were not what they seemed—brutal conquerors with an obsessive lust for gold—but were in truth Quetzalcoatl and his men reincarnated, and had returned to rule over the Aztec nation and the rest of mankind. The Spaniards, in telling contrast, were certain beyond doubt that their cause was not only profitable but noble and just.

Hernán Cortés sums up this conviction in one of the self-serving letters he wrote at discreet intervals throughout the conquest, to his sovereign, Charles V, king of Spain. The excerpt is from Cortés's third letter and sets out to explain how and why the conquistadors won one of their innumerable battles on the way to Tenochtitlán against numerically superior Indian forces.

As Cortés put it:

"We had just causes and good reasons on our side.

"One cause was because we fought for the spread of our Faith, and against barbarians.

"Another was because we served Your Majesty.

"Another was for the security of our lives.

"And another because we had many natives, our friends, to help us.

"All these were strong motives to animate our hearts. For the same reason I told them [the Spanish soldiers] to cheer up and be brave."

CHAPTER TEN

But the Floating Gardens Remain

THE Spaniards remained brave to the bitter end of the conquest and through the chaos that followed. But the cheers soon faded. The very qualities that made the Spaniards successful conquerors also made them terrible governors. In Mexico, as in every other part of the Americas they subdued, the Spaniards soon fell to bitter feuding among themselves, leading to devious politicking at the court of Castile and to nasty infighting in Mexico on the backs of the conquered Aztecs. Misery and ruthless exploitation became the general lot of the conquered, and grandiose pretensions, haunted at all times by rivalry and danger, became the fate of the conquerors. Even Cortés himself, indisputably the leader of the Spanish forces in the conquest, did not get what he wanted and what, by the standards of his time, was clearly his due: the governorship of Mexico. When the wrangling over the spoils was done, Cortés wound up on the sidelines as Marquis de Valle, lord of the Valley of Oaxaca, the domain of the Zapotecs and the Mixtecs. Tenochtitlán and the heartland of the Aztecs went to another Spaniard who had had no part in the conquest.

We know how the conquered Aztecs lived, felt and survived in the grim period that followed the conquest. We owe that knowledge to seventeen codices that were compiled by that first postwar generation. All of these codices were written in the Latin alphabet but the language used is either the Aztecs' own imperial tongue, Nahuatl, or Spanish. The illustrations in these codices also were the work of both Mexicans and Spaniards, but whoever the artists, the results are primitive. They reflect the brutishness of the period.

And yet, what the glory of the two empires, the Aztec and the Spanish, could not accomplish, the agony of the two peoples after the conquest finally achieved. They learned to understand each other. Slowly, gradually, they built a bridge between the two cultures that individuals could cross, and are heading now toward a fusion of the two peoples that has still not been completed.

Today, the population of Mexico consists about two-fifths of pure-blooded Indians, many of them living much as their ancestors did half a millennium ago. Only 5 percent of the people of Mexico are of purely European stock and the pride and prestige that used to be associated with this status is fading. The rest of the Mexican people, now constituting a clear majority, are of mixed ancestry and carry both in their genes and their values that amalgam of two races and two civilizations which Cortés and Montezuma briefly tried for, but tragically failed to achieve.

The amalgam is visible in many ways, in many places. It is most evident in the faces of today's Mexicans, which often display Aztec coloring with the acquilinity of classic

Spanish features, or offer the fascinating contrast of light eyes and the glossy blue-black of Indian hair.

The amalgam can be seen in structural form in such places as the Plaza of the Three Cultures in the heart of Mexico City, where the ruins of Tenochtitlán's mammoth market are flanked by a Franciscan church of the Spanish colonial period; a row of workers' houses built during the Mexican revolution of the first decade of this century; and the handsome modern building that houses the Foreign Office of the Federal Republic of Mexico. When that office has occasion to run up the flag, the colors are the strong primary hues that were featured in Aztec crafts and costumes. And the grand seal of Mexico has, at its center, the legendary Aztec eagle, perched on a cactus and holding Huitzilopochtli's serpent in its beak.

Other scenes illustrate the harmonization that has occurred over the centuries. Throughout Mexico, in remote villages as well as in the heart of big cities, open air markets continue to function much as they did in Aztec days. About three-fifths of the merchandise is exactly what it was five hundred years ago and the markets' purpose and style has altered even less. Today, as in Aztec times, the markets are organized along product lines, are orderly, and hum with activity and conversation. Now as then, they serve both as a place to exchange goods and a place to trade news. And now, as then, they display Mexican life in all its brilliance and variety. The breechclout and tunic have given way to shirt and trousers but the women's skirts and camisoles are still much as they used to be, and the spectacular attire of warriors and nobles of the old days survives in spirit in the silks and satins, the embroidered breeches or even the sequined and appliquéd blue jeans of the fashionable folk of today.

The most idyllic chord in the harmony that has been composed over the centuries is probably Xochimilco, the enchanting village not far from Mexico City, where the floating gardens of the Aztec days continue their fragrant existence. Xochimilco is threaded by canals that are replete with moss and water lilies and are traversed by painted canoes with colorful awnings, usually heaped with flowers. The flowers come from *chinampas,* mud islands that have been anchored with weeds, just as they were in Lake Texcoco when the Aztecs first settled there. When cultivated, as they still are in Xochimilco, these islands can produce three crops of corn a year or a profusion of flowers. Corn remains a staple of the Mexican diet in its classic form of patties (*tortillas* or the toasted *chacos*) and nowadays some of it is also turned into corn chips that are packed into plastic bags and shipped all over the world. The flowers are used for pigment as they were when the Aztec empire was at its zenith, and for decoration and delight, as both the Aztecs and the Spaniards used them when the Americas' grimmest and most disastrous encounter took place.

PART TWO

CHAPTER ELEVEN

The Life of a Girl Called Windflower and The Death of a Boy Named Hungry Coyote

TEOTIHUACÁN, the Place of the Gods, lay silent. A full moon flooded the sacred way, turned it into a stream of silver in the cloud-dark night. Moonbeams caressed cornices of the thirteen sanctuaries that lined the holy avenue, cast pewter-hued shadows over the 365 stone figures that stood guard over the temple complex, one figure for each day of the year. Beyond the sacred valley, two sierras clawed at the sky.

In the pitch-black sanctuary of the abandoned temple, a white-clad figure swayed before the stone frieze that had once been the altar of Tlaloc, the revered god of rain. Tapered fingers, strong and supple, held up a tiny vial of luminescent green.

"Bless this magic powder, oh Tlaloc," a woman's voice intoned, "to cool a fevered brow, as your raindrops cool the hot earth in the summer; to assuage limbs in pain as you assuage the parched ground in the spring; to bring the gentle peace of your liquid realm to a brave warrior who may be in need of it."

"Need of it," echoed the sanctuary's walls, "need of it, need of it."

When the last of the echoes had died, the raised hands withdrew and the woman stepped sideways ten measured paces. She stopped before a stone carving of Quetzalcoatl, the Feathered Serpent, guardian deity of the Aztec realm, and once more raised her hands in prayer. This time they cupped a small bag of earth-colored cotton.

"This is your secret, Quetzalcoatl," the woman whispered, "the sacred mushroom that can raise a man's spirit to meet you in your heavens, or plunge him into the horrors of hell. It is your most dangerous secret. We worship you for sharing it with us. I offer it for your blessing. Bless it with your wisdom."

"Wisdom," the echo repeated, "wisdom."

The dance of the echo had not yet ended when another rhythmic sound broke the silence of the sacred way. The woman turned, moved out of the sanctuary in long, liquid strides to the top of the pyramid terrace. She could hear a footfall, soft but steady, coming closer. Shading her eyes with her hands, she peered down the broad stairs into the silver path below, and saw him then, moving toward the temple.

He wore only an embroidered cotton breechclout and gem-encrusted sandals. Into the breechclout he had tucked his obsidian knife with its handle shaped like an eagle's head. The blade and the eagle's turquoise eyes gleamed. His hands, held out straight before him, clasped a bouquet of tall flowers. She recognized them in an instant. They were tall lilies from the island gardens of Xochimilco. They swayed as he moved, bowing, it seemed to her, in obeisance to the single tall feather he wore at the back of his head. It was the brilliant green-blue feather of a quetzal.

She dropped her hands from her eyes. A moonbeam caught the thick, blue-black braids wound around her head, and made them glint like a tiara. The braids were tied with colored ribbons, the colors repeated in the embroidery of her tunic and the hem of her long, flowing skirt. Her form was full, her features extraordinarily symmetrical.

She looks like a statue, he thought, the statue of a goddess. Of what? Of flowers and song? Of herbs and spices?

He remembered how the same thought, the same questions had crossed his mind the first time he saw her, at the court of Texcoco, when the prince had given audience to singers presenting their new poems and to priests offering new hymns. She sat very near the prince, in a group of priests, the only woman there. He had wondered who she was. She offered no song of her own: just sat there, throughout the music-filled night, symmetrical and serene. Like a statue.

But she wasn't a statue. Through fervid inquiries he discovered that she was a healer, so adept that Montezuma himself had commanded her services and she was now part of his retinue. As was he, a recently appointed member of the Eagle Knights, who vied with the Jaguar Knights for the glory of being the best warriors of the realm.

Our knives and spears will be tested soon, he thought, in the most important battle we have ever fought.

Had she read his thoughts? She had magic powers and no one knew where these powers began or ended.

When he reached the top of the stairs she said nothing but simply held out her hands, cradling a small vial and a tiny cotton bag in the hollow of her palms.

"I have brought these for you," she said, "rabbit's leg and sacred mushroom. You may have need of both."

He laid down the flowers on the top step of the pyramid, took the gifts she offered and put them beside the tall lilies.

"I am grateful you came," he said. "I was not certain the priest would tell you of my need."

"I am a healer," she replied. "Priests and princes know

this. And they know that the times are grave. Momentous events are before us. You have a part to play in these events. I will tell you the meaning and purpose of my gifts. But you must remember first what brought you to this point."

She lowered herself to sit beside the vial and the cotton bag, motioned him to take a place beside the flowers.

"Your home is in Xochimilco?" she inquired.

"I was born there. After I was born, for more than a week, the priests could not find an auspicious day for my naming ceremony. My parents were troubled. But when the day was finally fixed and the tools and weapons were put into my hammock, I reached for the weapons in a second and never looked at anything else. They tell me I held the arrow in my fingers for twenty-four hours and cried when they took it away."

"And then?"

"I am a farmer's son. Like everyone in Xochimilco, my clan grows flowers. As a child, I worked with my father as all sons do, but they sent me to the calmecac early. I never left the school after that, except to take part in battles, until the Knights of the Eagles accepted me in their ranks two years ago. I was only fourteen."

"But your name, Nazahualcoyotl, is a Texcoco name."

"Yes. I loved a girl in Xochimilco. But she belonged to my mother's clan and I could not marry her. She married a prince of Texcoco. I took the name of Texcoco's greatest king, Nezahualcoyotl, the famous, hunted hungry coyote, and swore to serve and protect her and her prince. Forever. And for many months, like a hungry coyote, I howled in the night. In silence. In my heart."

Her stern features softened. "I, too," she said, and her voice sounded blurred, remote, as if she were calling on lives long gone, memories long lost.

"I, too, troubled my parents when naming time came. I was born under the sign of Ehecatl, the wind and the whirlwind. I was named Quetzalxochitl, Windflower, but when they brought the implements for weaving and spinning on my naming day, I had just reached out to touch the little loom when a wind blew it out of my hands. It was a strong wind. The loom danced about the room and broke into seven pieces. There was great consternation. But the priest told my parents that seven pieces meant good luck. They wanted to know what kind of luck. He would not tell them."

Hungry Coyote looked startled.

"Why" he demanded.

Windflower lowered her head. Her voice sounded strangled.

"They were not worthy."

The young man's hand gripped the handle of his knife. This was vile disobedience. Blasphemy almost. Was she, after all, not a healer but a sorceress? He remembered a lesson he had been taught in the calmecac, over and over again. The ways to distinguish between a healer and a sorceress. It was very important to know that difference. Failure to distinguish could ruin one's life. How did the lesson go? Oh yes!

The healer: well versed in herbs.
Knows through experience
The roots, the trees, the stones.
She is experienced
Tests her remedies
Examines
Keeps her secrets, her traditions.
The good healer:
Cures people
Helps them
Puts them on their feet
Eases their bodies
Makes them recover
Covers their wounds with ashes, cures, remedies
Makes incisions

Draws the blood
Sews, purges people
Gives them remedies.

Was Windflower that? Or was she the other kind?

The bad healer:
Also has her traditions
Keeps them
Has her seeds, her powdered seeds
Possesses her charms, her flowers
Is like a spirit, a sorceress
Gives false remedies
Kills with them
Makes people worse
Places them in danger
Makes them sicken
Causes them to die.

What were the powders she had brought in that vial and that cotton bag?

He stared at them, moved away, saw a tear drop on his flowers.

"The calling came to me early," she whispered, "in dreams. I was taught the mysteries. How to find roots and herbs. The rituals that cure people. Once I spoke in my dream. About the rites. My father heard me. He was a merchant, just returned from a successful journey. He was giving a party to pay homage to Yacatehcutli, the god of the merchants, and to celebrate his own safe and profitable return. There were many men in the house. They had eaten and drunk a great deal. When he heard me speak in my sleep, my father came close to my mat and listened. And then went back to his party and repeated what he had heard. They did not believe him. They hardly heard what he said. They were all half dazed with spirits. But the priest of Yacatehcutli was there and he told the priest who had named me.

"The next night the priest who had named me came to fetch me from my parents' house. He took me on an expedition with other healers and priests which lasted until dawn. And then he brought me to the house of the priestesses that was attached to the court. I never went to my parents' home again."

Hungry Coyote's hand slipped from his knife.

Strange, he thought. How different her life has been from mine. And how much the same.

He reached for the little vial, nested it in his palm and held his hand out to her, much as she had done earlier.

"What is it you have brought me?" he inquired gently. "How will it help me? What purpose will it serve in what I must do to protect us all?"

She lifted her head and he could see her eyes still glistening with tears. But her voice was steady again and grave.

"It is the secret of Tlaloc. If you are wounded in battle, or if a friend is wounded and the pain is too much to bear, swallow the vial's contents. It will soothe the pain and ease your limbs. A veil like cotton gauze will flutter over your mind."

Hungry Coyote tilted his palm to drop the vial on the steps. It nearly shattered. His voice was sharp.

"Eagle Knights are trained to bear pain, not to obliterate it. Our minds in battle are acute, not veiled."

She reached out to righten the vial where it had fallen, and set it again beside the little cotton bag.

"Not all Aztecs are Eagle Knights," she said. "An ally may have need of it. Or a friend."

A sullen shadow settled on his face.

"Aztecs do not trade in forgetfulness. That comes soon enough. Our lives are short and filled with agony. They must have glory and beauty for balance. There is beauty in pain, glory in courage. Tlaloc's gifts are needed in Xochimilco. But I serve the Lords of Texcoco."

She smiled and pointed to the flowers.

"You came carrying these. When we first met, at the

court of Texcoco, poets and priests were weaving garlands, the garlands of the mind, poems and songs, and you sat enthralled all night. As did I."

"But these were songs to remember, not vapors to forget."

She laced her fingers.

"They are intertwined."

As if to illustrate her thought, a wind, warm but strong, drove some clouds over the face of the moon. The light that had enveloped them, and turned the sacred way into a silver swath, now cast patterns of darkness over their faces, over the temple steps on which they sat, over the Place of the Gods as far as they could see.

"Do you know the Tlalocan?" she asked. "Have you seen the painting of Tlaloc's paradise?"

He nodded.

"There is song and dance in Tlaloc's paradise. There are butterflies and blossoms, turtles and birds, fruit and feathers. There are men who play the ball game in Tlaloc's paradise and men who contemplate the universe. It is a place of many riches, many choices, many joys. You are wrong to be contemptuous of Tlaloc's blessings."

The sullen expression of his face changed to sadness.

"We have different tasks and duties, you and I," he said. "Our worlds are not the same. What you call joys, I call vanities. The riches of flowers are short-lived. They wither and die. So do blossoms and butterflies. And you and I. The sovereign whose name I bear sings it thus:

"The passing vanities of the world are like the green willow; it falls before the axe, is uprooted by the wind, is scarred and saddened by age.

"Life's splendors are like flowers whose color and whose fate they share.

"The beauty of flowers lasts only as long as their blossoms gather and store the precious pearls of dawn and let them fall in liquid dew.

"But when the Lord of All causes the sun to shine upon

them, their beauty and their glory fade.

"The reign of flowers is short. In the morning they boast of their beauty and strength, but by evening they mourn for the downfall of their thrones and the misfortunes that lead to loss, poverty, death and the grave.

"All things on earth come to an end, and in the midst of the happiest life our breath fails. We falter, and fall to earth."

He had recited the famous song of King Nezahualcoyotl of Texcoco, beginning it low and sad, but toward the end, as he sang of death, his voice had risen to a pitch of passion.

In her mind, as she listened, she heard a chorus of obsidian knives clashing, the whistling of arrows, the clatter of spear carriers discharging their weapons.

"Yes," she said. "That, too, is true. And therefore I have brought you the sacred mushroom, which helps you to see joy and splendor, death and the grave, and what lies beyond them all."

She pointed to the small, earth-colored sack and he reached for it quickly with both hands.

"It is the special secret of Quetzalcoatl," she said. "I asked him to bless it with his wisdom. Be careful how you make use of it."

He held it close to his chest. The sullenness and sadness had gone from his face. His eyes shone.

"I have heard that it gives visions of heaven," he said, "where the souls of brave warriors become stars that light up the firmament."

He looked up and she followed his gaze. The scudding clouds screened the stars scattered over the Place of the Gods, but beyond, above the sierras, they twinkled golden.

"It is a precious gift you have made me. I shall treasure it and use it with care."

She did not reply. A long silence fell between them.

When she spoke again, it was as if out of a deep reverie.

"Quetzalcoatl is returning to his people."

He blinked.

"Have you not heard of the *tules* with pink faces and golden hair who have come from the Eastern Sea?"

His body jerked to rigid attention.

"They are invaders."

She shook her head slowly.

"Invaders, perhaps. But they are not enemies. They come to fulfill the ancient prophecy. Quetzalcoatl, who walked into the sea in the dawn of our ancestors' time but promised to return, is returning now to lead us from war to peace. From courage to harmony. From power to wisdom."

For a moment, an expression of hope flashed across his face. Doubt chased it and then he shook his head violently.

"They have killed our vassals," he exploded, "they have turned against us the chiefs of tribes that pay tribute. They have stirred up our subjects, they have forged alliances with our enemies. They are marching now on Tenochtitlán. They mean to destory us, not to save us."

"No," she said. "The Lord Montezuma has had omens. They are Quetzalcoatl and his men returned to take up residence again in their true home. The Lord Montezuma will go to meet them when the time comes, and welcome them to their land."

His eyes opened wide and his voice carried both horror and disbelief. "The Lord Montezuma will leave his palace and travel the causeways to meet the invaders?"

"He will be carried in his little palace, the royal palanquin," she replied. "Nobles will sweep the causeways before him. And he will journey to bring the Feathered Serpent to Tenochtitlán."

The imperial palace and its grounds hummed with activity. The stately rhythm of Aztec nobles arriving to consult their lord, or to present vassal chiefs delivering tribute, was accompanied now by a different beat: the quicker pace of Spanish soldiers, in velvet or steel, their booted strides heavy and clamorous beside the soft tread of the sandal-shod members of Montezuma's court. The arboretum, usually an oasis of beauty and silence, with only trees and flowers whispering in the wind, now carried the sound of human voices, deep and resonant, sending forth round vowels and sibilant consonants. A section of the garden, near the guest palace that housed the Spaniards, had been turned into a sanatorium where the Spaniards took the sun, rested, had their boils lanced and their flesh wounds dressed and drank herb-tea when their roiled innards required soothing.

In that part of the garden, under the giant green umbrella of a ceiba tree, Windflower was sorting herbs and roots. She had separated them into several small mounds, spread around her in a semicircle. She sat in the circle's center, in a plain, loose, snow-white tunic and a skirt that reached to her ankles, her glossy hair parted and plaited in two heavy braids that reached nearly to the small of her back. Under her breath, she was humming a tune, which made a gray-haired Spanish soldier clattering by in his spurs stop short.

She was so absorbed, she did not notice him.

"Señorita," he said.

She looked up. He smiled.

"A lullaby," he commented. "It is the song my wife sang to our infant son when last I saw her."

Windflower shook her head and pointed to her lips to indicate that she could not speak the man's tongue. He nodded, cupped and swung his gnarled hands to indicate a cradle and, in his deep base voice, accompanied her in the song. They finished it together.

When he swung his hands, she had noticed that his knuckles were rubbed raw and that he had deep welts in the palms of his hands. She pointed to one of the mounds surrounding her and to a clay pot resting on a wood fire, then indicated his hands. He followed her gestures carefully with his eyes, then spoke in reply. She did not understand what he said but heard well the somewhat embarrassed, grateful tone of his voice. He pointed to the sun, and gestured to the west. She nodded. He would come back at dusk and she would dress his gaunt, bruised hands in a soft dressing of healing herbs. He would come back, she knew, each evening, and after a week his hands would be healed. She had applied her arts to more than a dozen Spanish soldiers, and they bowed to her now whenever they passed her.

Bowed, and . . .

Her face flushed as she remembered. One of her soldier-patients, a young man with eyes like jade and skin the color of sun-bleached corn but hair almost as dark and rich as her own, had brought a nosegay of flowers when he came to be treated the second time. He had held it out in front of him and she wondered how he had learned so quickly the customs of Montezuma's court. But instead of bending his own nose over it, he had offered the flowers to her. And when she had looked confused, he had bowed deeply and laid the bouquet at her feet.

That had happened before the second treatment. When a week had passed, and she had taken off the last of her leaf bandages from the deep gash on his cheek, which had knitted together again under her ministrations and was beginning to look pink and healthy, he had not only bowed deeply but picked up her hand and, before she could retrieve it or cry out, had raised it high and gently pressed his lips on its back. Then he had looked into her eyes and for a few seconds she had left her hand in his, her face crimson, her heart expanding in her chest. He had let go of her hand then, bowed again, and walked away. All this had happened only the day before, but it seemed to her as if it had been a dream, or a vision of a place far away and a time long ago.

During the preceding week, whenever she had brewed her herbed tea for his dressing, he had watched her, leaning against the trunk of the tree and softly sung the tune that kept reverberating in her mind. Now she knew that it was a song to lull infants to sleep. Its melody flowed through her. Once again she began to hum.

When the shadow fell upon the grass, she knew who it was without looking up. Cape and shield cast an unmistakable pattern, topped by the wood and feathers of a full, formal headdress of the Eagle Knights.

When she did look up, there was a frown on his smooth forehead and she saw the glitter of anger in his eyes. But his voice was even as he said:

"You sing the song of the strangers."

"They are Quetzalcoatl's emissaries."

He shook his head.

"I think not. But I have seen and heard perplexing happenings. They trouble me. I wish. I wish to. . . ." His voice trailed off and he lowered himself on the grass beside her.

"Yes, Hungry Coyote," she said gently.

His face was turned to her but his eyes seemed to look through and beyond her. His voice was thick.

"I was in Cholula. I fought with the men of Cholula against the invaders."

Her heart seemed to miss a beat, then race in her chest.

"And?"

"And they won. I do not understand how. We had planned very carefully. There were many of us. But they seemed to know what we had in mind before we could execute our plan. And although they were few, they killed hundreds with those fighting sticks they have that speak lightning and thunder."

"Were you hurt? Did you make use of the rabbit's leg?"

He shook his head.

"No. I escaped. I offered the rabbit's leg to a Tlaxcalan who was wounded very badly. But he would not accept it."

"Why? Did you tell him it would ease the pain?"

"I did. But he said he could bear the pain, he was a Tlaxcalan. And the Spaniards would take care of him."

"The Spaniards? Take care of him?"

"Yes. Him and his family, his clan, his people. He was convinced of it."

"What made him so certain?"

"He said he had seen them fight, almost from the beginning, soon after they arrived in those houses of theirs that float on the water. He said when he saw them first they were mounted on their giant deer with whom they move as one. And they fought like gods.

"That's what he said. And then his breath stopped and his soul flew from him."

"And you?"

"I went to a temple nearby to commend his soul to Huitzilopochtli. But he was not there."

"Huitzilopochtli was not there?"

"No. His sanctuary had been charred. His image had been toppled. And in its place stood two tall sticks crossed at the top."

He showed her, raising one index finger and laying the other over it to make the shape of the cross.

"The strangers say this is the sign of heaven. They kneel before it and bow their heads."

A picture of the young Spanish soldier flashed through Windflower's mind. He had arrived under the ceiba tree one day not in steel but in velvet, with a sign like the one Hungry Coyote described, hung on a chain around his neck. And when she had pointed to it, questioning with her eyes, he had lifted it to the sky and kissed it, gently, as he had kissed her hand.

Heat rushed to her cheeks. She lowered her face to make certain Hungry Coyote did not see her trembling. But his mind was far away.

"I met some Cholulans in that temple," he recounted. "They had come with a prisoner whom they wanted to sacrifice. But the priests had gone, along with Huitzilopochtli. They did not know what to do. They asked me for counsel."

"And what did you tell them?"

"I told them to leave the prisoner under the strangers' heavenly sign. And we would see what would happen."

"They did this?"

"Yes. And I kept vigil nearby. The Cholulans returned the next day. The prisoner was dead. Perhaps the gods of the strangers took his heart during the night. I did not see them.

But then the strangers say their god cannot be seen."

"And what happened to the men of Cholula who had brought him for sacrifice?"

"They were distraught. I tried to comfort them. I cited the wise words of my namesake."

"What did you say?"

"I told them that the whole earth is a grave. Nothing escapes. Nothing is so perfect that it will not fail and disappear. The rivers, brooks, fountains and waters flow onward and never return to their source. They hurry to the vast immaterial kingdom, and the broader their banks, the swifter they reach the tomb. What was yesterday, is not today. That which is today, may not be tomorrow."

"Were they comforted by the words of Nezahualcoyotl?"

"Somewhat. But they wanted to know what would happen. To them. To the Aztec empire."

"And did you answer their questions?"

His voice was deep in his throat.

"I told them what Nezahualcoyotl had said, generations ago. That the caves of the earth are full of lowly dust that once was bone and flesh, the bodies of kings enthroned. Once they judged and ruled, governed and conquered, piled treasure upon treasure, razed temples to the ground. They vaunted themselves with pride and ostentation, wealth and flattery and power. These glories have passed like the dark smoke belched by the fires of the volcano. They leave no trace, only the parchment on which the record is written."

"And did this allay their confusion?"

"In due measure. But they wanted to know what would the parchment record of this time, the time of the strangers in our land."

"And how did you answer?"

"Again, with the words of Nezahualcoyotl."

"Which of his many wise words?"

"These: if I were to lead you into the depth of the temple, if I were to ask you which of these bones were our kings, what would you reply? You would say, as I do, I know not; I know not. For the greatest and the least are confounded in common clay. Their fate shall be our fate and the fate of all who come after."

Hungry Coyote's voice trailed off and his eyes returned from the far distance to which they had been fixed. He looked at Windflower.

"Is this not true about the strangers also?"

She met his gaze.

"Perhaps. The Lord Montezuma went out to meet them on the causeway. They touched his venerable person. They hung a garland of jewels around his neck. The chief of the strangers dismounted from his giant deer and greeted the Lord Montezuma on the ground, when our Lord had alighted from his palanquin. They were the same height, our Lord and the chief of the strangers. They spoke to each other with affection.

"How do you know this?"

"There is a woman with the strangers from the coast of the east, who speaks their tongue. She told me, after she saw how I dressed their wounds."

Hungry Coyote looked at the mounds of roots and herbs surrounding Windflower. Then he saw one of the strangers, a young man, his own age perhaps, walk toward them and stop when he realized Windflower was not alone. And he saw Windflower's cheek become pink with the rising blood, then pale.

"You dress their wounds and sing their songs."

It was a statement. His voice was harsh and flat as he made it. She nodded.

"You have been to the palace where they stay?" he demanded.

"No. But our Lord Montezuma is with them."

"I have heard this. They have made him a prisoner."

"No." She shook her head violently.

"He is their guest. He will return to his palace when he knows for certain that they are Quetzalcoatl and his men."

Hungry Coyote gripped his shield so hard the knuckles

rose sharp and taut like points of an arrow.

"The Lord Montezuma will never know," Hungry Coyote hissed through clenched teeth.

"The Lord Montezuma will never again leave the strangers' palace."

A veil of smoke and reeking fumes obscured the sun as it rose over the ruins of Tenochtitlán. The early morning air hung heavy over the vast market place at the foot of the main temple of the Aztec capital. No merchants plied their trade. The market was fetid, stank of blood and rotting corpses, and the oozing wounds of the hurt and maimed.

Some of these wounded lay, sat, or crawled under what was left of a market arcade. Against the wall, using it to prop her up, Windflower hunched over her plants and herbs, preparing bandages. Her face was thin, drawn with fatigue, emaciated by hunger. Her hair fell to her shoulders, open and matted with mud and blood. Her skirt and tunic were tattered and caked with dirt.

She did not notice him at first. In her weary mind, he was just another body, painfully pulling himself from the bottom of the temple steps across the expanse of the market grounds in the heat of the early but already turgid day. When she looked again, her heart froze. Was it perhaps not another Indian soldier but a giant bird, an eagle, coming to devour them all? But no, those were human eyes, deeply sunken in their sockets and alive with agony, that peered out between the full-length armor of an eagle knight and the headdress pulled down low over the forehead. The hands were empty. He did not carry a spear hurtler, nor a bow and arrow, nor even a fighting stick. He used his hands to push himself forward, on his belly, across the market, toward the arcade.

She pulled him the last stretch, reaching under his arms. As she did so, she felt the hot blood seep through the padded cotton. When she had succeeded in laying him on a straw mat near her—it was frayed and dirty, but it was a mat—and felt his heart, the beat was still there, and regular, but very faint.

His voice was a whisper.

"It is good to see you."

It was an effort for him to speak.

She removed the headdress, put a gentle hand on his brow.

"I have been in Texcoco most of the time since last we met," she said.

A shadow of pain crossed his face.

"I know."

"You know?"

"I was there myself, for a short time. A very short time. And I heard."

"What did you hear?"

"I heard that you had returned to help the conquerors build their ships. And that you were bearing a child. My child."

Windflower's voice fell to a whisper as low as his.

"Yes. That is what I told my parents. You must forgive me. In Tenochtitlán, I married a Spaniard. The child is ours, his and mine. But during the sad night I fled with him, and we were parted in the terrible chaos. I was heavy with child and did not know where to go. So I went home to my parents. I knew that if I told them the baby was that of an eagle knight, they would be pleased. And they would take care of it. And of me. They did. The child is with them now."

"That, too, I was told, when I was in Texcoco."

"But what took you there? Were you not sworn to fight the conquerors?"

"I was. But I had heard that my prince had changed loyalty. That he was aiding them, supporting the conquest. I wanted to know why."

"Did you find out?"

"Yes. I spoke with him. He said that the Aztecs had been brutal and selfish. That Tenochtitlán was doomed and deserved to be. That the conquerors were men of valor and honor, and many skills, who would bring a new dawn to the land and to all the peoples who had lived under the night of Aztec rule."

"Did he say that they were Quetzalcoatl and his men, returned to us as promised?"

"No, he did not. But he told me that he had talked to some of their priests and that these priests believed in a spirit, unseen and universal, who created all and to whom everything returned. As my namesake Nezahualcoyotl believed—and sang—a hundred years ago. So the prince said. And he asked me to take off my Eagle Knight's armor and stay in the court of Texcoco."

"And did you do that?"

"No. I am an Eagle Knight. In my dreams, I see the cactus on the island of reeds where it all began, and I hear the screech of the eagle holding the snake in its beak. This beginning is my beginning. Its end will be my end."

She opened his armor, saw the deep wound in his side. Carefully, she laid an herbed bandage over the gash. He closed his eyes and a look of rest settled on his face.

"You must go to Xochimilco when it is finished," he said. "Tell my parents what you told yours in Texcoco. They will care for you and the child. It will be finished soon."

She looked around her. Destruction and havoc as far as the eye could see: the market, the causeways, the houses, broken and silent. Only at the very top of the temple, there was still an ear-splitting clash of weapons, the conquerors' iron, the defenders' wood and stone, the drums, the yells and howls, the dull thud of bodies falling, wounded or dead. Dead mostly.

Her voice was hoarse and sad.

"No," she said, "I cannot. I must find my husband and stay with him; or go wherever he goes."

He opened his eyes.

"You will join him when the time has come. Not yet."

She stared down at him.

"You know my husband?"

"Yes."

It was difficult for him to speak, but he drove himself to the effort.

"When the leader of the conquerors went away to the coast and left behind in Tenochtitlán the Cruel One with the red beard, I was in the city. I was there when the Cruel One massacred the nobles and priests in the temple. And I saw the anger of some of his fellow-soldiers when he returned to his camp on that sad night. One who was angry was very young, with white skin and green eyes and hair like yours. When I asked who he was and why he was angry, I was told that he had a Texcoco healer for wife, whom he held dear. I remembered then that he had watched us from afar when I talked with you in Montezuma's garden. And later I saw him again."

"Where? When?"

His voice strengthened with an undertone of triumph.

"On what *they* call the sad night. When we drove them out of the city and they fled, using their bodies and the bodies of their giant deer to make bridges over which to flee. I saw him try to put you on his big animal and take you away with him, but his leader would not allow it and you remained behind."

"Yes," she said, tonelessly. It was the last time she had seen him.

His voice fell again, lower, sadder than her own.

"I saw him once more."

Her eyes pleaded.

"It was last night. On the highest step of the temple. He was in great pain."

Her hands cramped around a clay pot simmering herbed liquid. The pot was scorching her fingers, but she did not notice it.

"I poured into his mouth the rabbit's leg you gave me in Teotihuacán. See."

He pointed to a small pouch stitched to his breechclout

beneath the armor. She reached and found the green vial. She tilted it into her hand. It was empty.

"He felt better very quickly. The pain went from his eyes. He went to the house of spirits—to the house of his spirit—with a smile on his face."

He pointed to the pouch once more.

"The sacred mushroom is with me still."

She reached down and found it quickly. The little brown bag was unharmed. It rested in her hand, round, weighty, secure.

Just holding it gives me a feeling of peace, she thought. How can that be? My husband is dead.

A dull pain suffused her.

Pain and peace, her mind echoed. Peace and pain. It will be like that for a very long time.

He stirred on the pallet beside her. Keeping his eyes on the palm of her hand that held the powder of the sacred mushroom, he put her other hand on his heart. Its beat was very faint and getting fainter.

"Not much longer" he murmured. "I will join the spirit of your husband before you do."

"Perhaps," she said. And her mind throbbed: peace and pain; pain and peace.

His voice cut through the drums in her head. "Give me the mushroom."

It was an order.

"The time has come."

She did not try to dissuade him. She opened the bag, held up his head with her arm and slowly sprinkled the powder on his tongue. Then she cupped her hand, poured some of the herb tea into her palm, allowed the tea to cool, and, drop by drop, let it fall into his mouth. Slowly, with a great last effort, he swallowed powder and liquid.

Suddenly, his eyes glowed. He sat up like a stretched bow, his two forefingers pointing to the sky.

Was he pointing to the temple, she wondered, or to the heavens? or both?

"Your husband fought bravely," he said. "They were like gods, there on the steps of the temple. Perhaps they are Quetzalcoatl and his men. Soon I will know for sure."

Her eyes were riveted to his chest, upright now, with the blood pouring from the wound.

Peace and pain, her own blood throbbed at her temples. Pain and peace.

"Nezahualcoyotl," he shouted. "I come to you, my ancestor, my illustrious forebear."

He looked around wildly.

"Warriors," he trumpeted to the wounded men lying in the arcade and scattered on the market grounds beyond.

"Warriors! Princes unconquered! Let us seek, let us sigh for heaven. All is eternal there. Nothing is corruptible. The blackness of the tomb is the sun's womb and the dark night shines with bright stars. No one has power to put out the lights of heaven, for they tell of the greatness of their maker.

"As our eyes behold them today, so did our fathers, and so shall our sons, forever."

His voice broke. He fell back, his head thudding on the floor. She felt his heart. It had stopped. She closed his eyes.

I will go to Xochimilco, she thought, and bring the child to Hungry Coyote's parents. And I will raise it there, among the flowers, with pain in my heart always for its father, and peace descending on me whenever I remember Hungry Coyote, the Eagle Knight. And some day, Quetzalcoatl will return to us all.

At the top of the temple stairs, the sanctuary of Huitzilopochtli crumbled. Church bells began to peal.

Windflower rose, turned, and walked away, south, toward Xochimilco.

PART THREE

CHAPTER TWELVE

Finding the Feathered Serpent

THE plumage of the Feathered Serpent is scattered all over Mexico, south as far as Guatemala, north to the borders of Arizona. Mexico alone, it is estimated, has some 10,000 archeological sites, the overwhelming majority still unexplored. These sites date back to the beginning of man in the Americas, a period that is now calculated to have been somewhere between 20,000–10,000 B.C. The sites bear witness to all the great civilizations that budded, flourished, and decayed in a time span encompassing some 4,000 years of human history and accomplishment in North America.

Much, therefore, remains to be uncovered by people with the curiosity, the particular sense of adventure, and the resources that are required for these journeys of exploration into the past.

The Olmecs seem to have a well-organized, well-run society. This is an assembly of Olmec citizens.

Such journeys are being made by someone, somewhere, each year. In the early 1970s, venturers into the past uncovered both the summer palace of Cortés, which had been unknown until then, and a major Aztec temple site at Cholula, with pyramids so ambitious in scale they match the pyramids of Egypt. On the campus of the National University of Mexico, a clumsy, small temple site mutely reminds today's searching students how far back the aspirations of their ancestors date. That site is calculated to be some 3,000 years old. And almost everywhere in Mexico City, when bulldozers or electric shovels chew up the present surface of the city, they unearth temples and markets, palaces, schools, residences and altars of the times of Tenochtitlán.

To appreciate the Feathered Serpent in all its complexity and brilliance, it should be viewed from at least half a dozen vantage points.

The first is La Venta, a lush paradise near the town of Villahermosa in the state of Tabasco, where an original Olmec site has been beautifully transplanted from the swampy coast on which it was discovered. The place is awash with the mystery and grace of Olmec wisdom and beauty, haunted by the sweep of Olmec power. Scattered on the site are giant Olmec heads in their baffling helmets; gaunt Olmec figures in counsel; stone carvings of men with African, Semitic and Egyptian features. La Venta displays the enigmatic Olmec jaguar's paws and face, and the laughing, fat-bellied Olmec babies; the famous "yokes," illustrating acrobatic feats the Olmecs must have been able to perform. At La Venta you can see an American world well over 3,000 years old: organized, complex, infinitely challenging to the mind and to the imagination, the beginning of the intellect and spirit that created the Feathered Serpent.

The second vantage point is Teotihuacán, which to the Aztecs became "The Place of the Gods." It is a beautifully proportioned temple site about thirty miles from Mexico City, with a sacred way leading from the Temple of the Sun

to the Temple of the Moon, and the intriguing remains of sanctuaries with calendric meaning, placed in mathematically calculated spaces along that broad, ancient avenue. The feeling one gets from the symmetry of the site, and the harmony built into the sacred way, is comparable to the sentiment that envelops a visitor to the Parthenon of the Greeks at Athens. Teotihuacán has carvings of the Feathered Serpent on altar friezes inside the Temple of the Sun, where Quetzalcoatl holds sway alongside Tlaloc, the rain god. In ancient palace grounds nearby are restored frescoes of Tlaloc's paradise, painted on the walls of the gracious villa of a royal resident of old Teotihuacán.

The third vantage point is in Oaxaca, which has remnants of both the Mixtec and the Zapotec civilizations, at the intriguing sites of Mitla and Monte Albán. The two sites span at least a millennium of pre-Columbian civilization and speak compellingly of the achievements of the two peoples in both the arts and the sciences. They demonstrate as well the particular contribution the Mixtecs and Zapotecs made to the brilliance of concept and color that became the Feathered Serpent.

The fourth view is from the Maya sites of Yucatán and the southern rainforest, where subtle architecture, beautiful sculpture, and paintings show dramatically how one great American civilization developed from the seed sown by the Olmecs. Maya art has its own version of the Feathered Serpent, and Maya literature tells the story of a mythical hero, part god, part man, who once brought skills and wisdom to the Maya people, then disappeared into the sea with the promise to return.

A fifth view is the Toltec version of the Feathered Serpent, which already contains much of the aggressive, warlike spirit that infused the Aztecs. It is best seen in Tula, a trip of about fifty miles from Mexico City. In Tula, giant Toltec stone soldiers gaze grimly at a sacrificial altar in a central courtyard of what once was a temple complex. The stone soldiers clasp their spear carriers to their sides with

There is no mistaking this typically realistic Aztec sculpture of a cat.

ramrod rigidity, but their breastplates are giant butterflies, another version of the serpent's feathers. And the soldiers' sandals are festooned with snakes. At Tula, Toltec monuments hark back to Olmec origins with carvings of jaguars, and foreshadow Aztec successors with friezes of ferocious eagles.

The most comprehensive view of the Feathered Serpent and its soaring history can be had in the heart of Mexico City, in the incomparable National Museum of Anthropology and History in Chapultepec Park. There, the history of humanity in the Americas begins with a skeleton 20,000 years old, the Man of Tepexpan, surrounded by his animal companions of that time: mamut and bison, peacock, heron, and turkey. Exhibits in the museum trace the history of American man from those beginnings to the days of Montezuma's glory and defeat. In the center of the museum, on a specially designed pedestal, glows a copy of the brilliant, green-blue headdress Montezuma wore when he encountered Cortés. It is wrought of the feathers of the quetzal.

And Some Expert Guides

Whether you decide to look for the Feathered Serpent by going to Mexico or by staying home, expert guides are at your disposal between the covers of books to point the way.

The very best of the guides is probably Bernal Díaz del Castillo, the tough and brave soldier, shrewd and meticulous observer, who fought with Cortés from the day he landed in Veracruz until Mexico was not only conquered but subdued. Captain Díaz describes battles and cities, sites and customs, accomplishments and personalities on both sides of the historic encounter. And he does so in brisk, lucid prose. Fortunately, the diaries he kept and the notes he made have been perfectly preserved and are available in English, under the title *The Bernal Díaz Chronicles,* translated and edited by Albert Idell and published by Doubleday and Co., Inc., New York. There is a paperback edition under the Dolphin Books imprint.

Interesting, but considerably more limited and more partisan, are the letters Hernán Cortés wrote to the court of Castile. They, too, have been preserved intact and exist in English translation under the title *Letters from Mexico,* translated and edited by A. R. Pagden, and published by Orion Press, New York.

A number of other conquistadors wrote eye-witness accounts, some dramatic and perceptive, some clumsy and self-serving. A vivid selection of such first-person writing is contained in a handsomely produced volume called *The Conquistadors,* edited, translated, and introduced by Patricia de Fuentes, and published by Orion Press, New York. The selection offers excerpts from the chronicles of the conquistadors Juan Díaz, Andrés de Tapia, and García del Pilar, and from the accounts of Father Francisco de Aguilar, who accompanied the Spanish conquerors. The book also contains Cortés's third letter to the emperor of Spain and two letters by Pedro de Alvarado, who perpetrated the massacre of the Aztecs in Tenochtitlán while Cortés was away, and who later crushed the Maya and became the first Spanish governor of Guatemala.

Another Spanish priest writing in the sixteenth century, mixing fact and myth, observation and speculation in a fascinating manner, was Father Diego Durán, a Dominican friar who came to Mexico shortly after the conquest had been completed. His account, *The Aztecs: The History of the Indies of New Spain,* was edited and translated in the 1960s by Doris Heyden and Fernando Horcasitas and published by Orion Press, New York. The book has an interesting introduction by Ignacio Bernal, curator of Mexico's National Museum of History and Anthropology, and director of the Mexican National Institute of Anthropology and History, himself one of the most profound experts on the Aztecs and their predecessors.

Father Durán had a fellow friar whose contribution to our knowledge of the Feathered Serpent matches, and in some ways surpasses, that of Fray Durán. The other cleric, Fray Bernardino de Sahagún, compiled a painstaking and occasionally searing account of the Aztecs as he encountered and observed them. It consists of thirteen volumes but is called simply, and accurately, *A General History of the Things of New Spain.* It is known also, and better, as *The Florentine Codex,* because it found its way to Europe and, early in the nineteenth century, was discovered in Florence. The Florentine Codex is of particular interest because it is illustrated, by Aztec artists, who depict with the simplicity and accuracy of a comic strip some of the manners and customs of their people as described by Father Sahagún. An English version of the major parts of the Florentine Codex has been edited and translated by Charles E. Dibble and Arthur J. O. Anderson, and published by the University of Utah at Salt Lake City.

The people of the Feathered Serpent themselves had no written language and therefore left no accounts of their own. They did, however, tell their stories to some sympathetic Spaniards who wrote down what they were told, during and after the conquest, usually with some distortions of their own, but always reflecting a great deal of Aztec fact and Aztec sentiment. Some of these books were illustrated by Aztecs, and that adds to their verisimilitude.

These accounts, written by Spaniards and illustrated by Aztecs, are known as codices. Seventeen of them exist, as far as we know. They are scattered all over the world, carefully kept in museums and libraries. A few have been translated and published in English. The Florentine Codex is one, the Mendoza Codex another. The Mendoza Codex was published in London just before World War II, as translated and edited by James Cooper Clark.

The most recently published codex in English translation is *The Codex Nutall: A Picture Manuscript from Ancient Mexico,* edited by Nelia Nutall, with an introduction by Arthur G. Miller, who is an archeologist at the Center for Pre-Columbian Studies at Dumbarton Oaks, near Washington, D.C. The Nutall Codex also surfaced in Florence, in a monastery, sometime in the nineteenth century. The English version, with beautifully reproduced illustrations, mainly by Mixtec artists, is published by Dover Publications, New York.

Writing about the Feathered Serpent 300 years later, in the second and in the fourth quarter of the nineteenth century, two guides are particularly appealing. One is Hubert Howe Bancroft, who reconstructed in painstaking and imaginative detail his version of the Mexican conquest and of the lives of the Aztec people before and immediately after the conquest. He did the former in a three-volume work entitled *The Conquest of Mexico,* published in New York in 1883, and the latter in a five-volume opus called *The Native Races,* published in San Francisco also in 1883. Both works are available in later editions in most U.S. public libraries that have a good collection of works dealing with pre-Columbian America.

Equally imaginative and romantic, in a very different way, is the account of the New England historian William H. Prescott, who wrote *The Conquest of Mexico,* a three-volume work that saw its first publication in 1843, in New York. It has been published in several versions and several places since then. The most accessible edition now is that of the Modern Library, called *History of the Conquest of Mexico.* It is a swashbuckling tale, both dramatic and philosophical, that makes finding the Feathered Serpent the kind of stirring adventure it ought to be.

Glossary

A Note on Pronunciation
a is pronounced ah, as in *a*rt
e is pronounced ay, as in *e*nd
i is pronounced ee, as in *i*s
o is pronounced oh, as in p*o*t
u is pronounced oo, as in b*u*ll
x is pronounced sh, as in *sh*adow
j is pronounced h′, as in the Scottish lo*ch*
ch is pronounced as in *ch*ildren, not as in choral
c is pronounced k, as in *k*ing, at the beginning of a word, but becomes s, as in *s*entence, in the middle of a word
qu is pronounced k, as in *k*ettle
hu is pronounced w, as in *w*ater
All vowels are pronounced separately, as in ch*ao*s.

ATLATL—A spear-thrower that was the Aztecs' notorious long-distance weapon.

CALMECAC—A special school for talented children.

CALPULLI—The Aztecs' basic social unit, composed of 50 to 100 families.

CHAC MOL—A stone figure that served as the special altar on which human sacrifice was offered.

CHALCHIUIS—Precious and semiprecious stones used by the Aztecs as jewelry.

CHICHA—A beer made of fermented maize.

CHINAMPA—A man-made island of weed-anchored mud, used by the Aztecs to grow grain, vegetables and, particularly, flowers.

CHIRIMOYA—A juicy fruit, consumed in Aztec times, still available in Mexico today.

CIHUACOATL—A judge who presided over the Aztecs' highest court, which also served as a council of state.

COPIL—An Aztec word for the long-spined, tough-fibered cactus that grows in Mexico. It was used by the Aztecs for a number of purposes.

CUICALLI—The word means "House of Song." It was the assembly hall in Aztec schools.

NAHUATL—The Aztecs' language.

NOPAL—Another Aztec word for cactus. *See* COPIL

POCHTECA—The merchants of the Aztec Empire. They were a separate class, with their own gods, courts, and privileges.

PULQUE—The fermented juice of the maguey plant, distilled to a high potency.

TEACHCAUTIN—The word means "oldest relative." He was the civil leader of the Aztecs' basic social unit. (There was also a military leader.)

TECALLI—The Aztecs' second highest court, in permanent session in Tenochtitlán.

TECHUHTLI—The military leader of the basic social unit.

TECPILLATOLLI—A very precise, refined, and stylized form of the NAHUATL language, used at court, in rhetoric, and in poetry.

TELPOCHCALLI—The word means "house of youth." They were the equivalent of grade schools in Aztec society, educating both boys and girls, although separately and in different subjects.

TEJOCOTE—An Aztec fruit, still available in Mexico today.

TEUCTLI—A community judge, elected for one year, who ruled on local civil and criminal cases.

TLACXITLAN—The Aztecs' supreme court, which doubled as a state council.

TLAMACAZQUI—A parish priest.

TLAMACAZTON—A seminary graduate, serving as a novice.

TLANAMACAC—A senior priest, equivalent to a Monsignor in the Catholic Church.

TLAPIZCATZITZIN—The word means "conserver." It designated special priests in charge of preserving the Aztecs' poetic traditions. These priests functioned as critics, teachers and censors of poetry.

TLAQUETZQUI—The word means "one who makes things stand out." A rhetoretician.

TLATOCAN—The word means "a place of discourse." It was the Aztecs' equivalent of a town meeting.

TLAXILACALLI—The word means "blocks of houses." An Aztec neighborhood.

TULES—The Aztecs' word for the Spaniards.

XICTOMATL—The Aztec word for tomato, which is a native American product.

Some Important Place Names

AZTATLAN—"The Place of the Cranes," the Aztecs' native island.

BONAMPAK—Site of a famous Maya temple, in the state of Chiapas, southern Mexico.

CHAPULTEPEC—The word means "Hill of the Grasshopper." It

was the source of water for the Aztec capital, and is now Mexico City's central park.

CHOLULA—An important city in the Aztec empire, one of the first to fight the Spaniards. Site of a major pyramid.

LA VENTA—An important site of Olmec artifacts, in the state of Tabasco.

MITLA—A major site of the Mixtec civilization, near Oaxaca.

MONTE ALBÁN—A multi-layered site, with fascinating remnants of the Olmec, Mixtec, and Zapotec civilizations. Near Oaxaca.

OAXACA—Largest city in southern Mexico, near the important sites of Mitla and Monte Albán.

TENOCHTITLÁN—Capital of the Aztecs. Its central plaza is now the main square of Mexico City.

TEOTIHUACÁN—"The Place of the Gods," the major site of "the father civilization" of Mexico, located just outside Mexico City.

TLATELOLCO—A city state conquered by the Aztecs late in the fifteenth century. Also the site of "The Declaration of Tlatelolco," which calls for new forms of cooperation in the Americas in the twentieth century.

TULA—An important site of the Toltec civilization.

VERACRUZ—On Mexico's east coast, the original landing place of the conquistadors.

VILLAHERMOSA—In the state of Tabasco, where La Venta, with its magnificent Olmec artifacts, is located.

YUCATÁN—The peninsula in eastern Mexico, with important Maya and Toltec sites.

XOCHIMILCO—A village outside Mexico City, threaded by waterways, where flowers are still grown on *chinampas.*

Index